DK | Penguin Random House

US Senior Editors Rebecca Warren, Margaret Parrish
US Editor Kate Johnsen
Senior Editors Shaila Brown, Daniel Mills, Ben Morgan, Rupa Rao
Senior Art Editors Vicky Short, Smiljka Surla
Editors Lizzie Munsey, Sam Priddy, Alison Sturgeon, Deeksha Saikia
Designers Daniela Boraschi, Tannishtha Chakraborty, Richard Horsford, Hedi Hunter, Fiona Macdonald
Visualizer Peter Laws
Illustrators Peter Bull, Rob Cook, FOREAL™, Mike Garland, Mark Garlick, ary Hanna, Jason Harding, Arran Lewis, Maltings Partnership, Medi-Mation, eter Minister, Gerson Mora and Anna Luiza Aragão/Maná e.d.i., Moonrunner Design, Ian Naylor, Alex Pang, Dean Wright and Agatha Gomes
DK Picture Library Emma Shepherd, Rob Nunn
Jacket Design Development Manager Sophia MTT
Jacket Designer Dhirendra Singh
Producers, pre-production Francesca Wardell, Jacqueline Street
Producer Ed Kneafsey
Managing Editors Julie Ferris, Paula Regan, Lisa Gillespie
Managing Art Editor Owen Peyton Jones
Publishers Sarah Larter, Andrew Macintyre
Design Director Phil Ormerod
Associate Publishing Director Liz Wheeler
Publishing Director Jonathan Metcalf
Special Sales and Custom Publishing Manager Michelle Baxter
Contributors Kim Bryan, Robert Dinwiddie, Jolyon Goddard, Ian Graham, Reg G. Grant, Jacqueline Mitton, Darren Naish, Douglas Palmer, Philip Parker, Penny Preston, Sally Regan, David Rothery, Carole Stott, Paul Sutherland, Chris Woodford, John Woodward

Content previously published as *Knowledge Encyclopedia* in 2013

First American Edition, 2016
Published in the United States by DK Publishing,
345 Hudson Street, New York, New York 10014

16 17 18 19 20 10 9 8 7 6 5 4 3 2
001–299207–July/16

A catalog record for this book is available from the Library of Congress.

ISBN: 978-5-0010-1426-3

‹ books are available at special discounts when purchased in bulk for sales romotions, premiums, fund-raising, or educational use. For details, contact: DK Publishing Special Markets, 345 Hudson Street, New York, New York 10014 or SpecialSales@dk.com

Printed and bound in China

A WORLD OF IDEAS:
SEE ALL THERE IS TO KNOW

www.dk.com

Smithsonian Institution

THE SMITHSONIAN

Established in 1846, the Smithsonian—the world's largest museum and research complex—includes 19 museums and galleries and the National 'oological Park. The total number of artifacts, works of art, and specimens the Smithsonian's collection is estimated at 137 million. The Smithsonian is a renowned research center, dedicated to public education, national service, and scholarship in the arts, sciences, and history.

THE MODERN WORLD

CONTENTS

The Age of Discovery 2
Voyage to the Americas 4
Ancient Americas 6
The Renaissance 8
Imperial China 10
Rulers of India 12
The modern world 14
The slave trade 16
The Enlightenment 18
The American Revolutionary War 20
The French Revolution 22
The Industrial Revolution 24
The Civil War 26
World War I 28
World War II 30
The Cold War 32
The 21st century 34

Index and Acknowledgments 36

THE AGE OF DISCOVERY

The world experienced huge changes between 1450 and 1750. A wave of new ideas swept across Europe as explorers founded new colonies and trading networks all across the world. European rivals often went to war with each other, and with the powerful empires of Asia, in the scramble for new territory.

NEW WAYS OF THINKING

In the medieval period, the Christian Church controlled art and learning in Europe. This changed around 1450 when important works by Greek and Roman authors were rediscovered and became popular. Scholars such as Erasmus (1466–1536) created a new movement called humanism, teaching that art and science should be based on experiment and observation rather than old traditions.

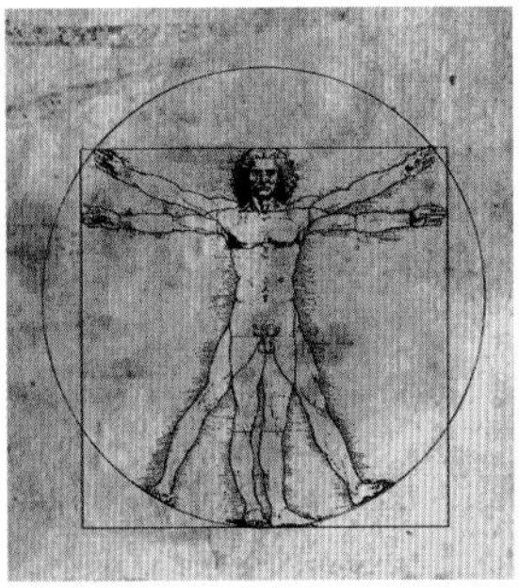

The Renaissance

A great deal of Roman art and architecture survived in Italy around 1400. It inspired artists, such as Michelangelo, Leonardo da Vinci, and Raphael, and architects, such as Brunelleschi, to produce daring new works of their own. Their artistic movement is called the Renaissance, and it soon spread across Europe.

Vitruvian Man
Renaissance artists such as Leonardo da Vinci studied human anatomy carefully to make their art as realistic as possible.

The Reformation

In 1517, a German priest called Martin Luther attacked the wealth of the Church and the right of the Pope to decide what people should believe. This movement–the Reformation–created a split between traditional Christians (Catholics) and supporters of Luther, called Protestants.

"WHY DOES THE POPE NOT BUILD [CHURCHES] **WITH HIS OWN MONEY,** RATHER THAN WITH THE MONEY OF POOR **BELIEVERS?"**
MARTIN LUTHER

Scientific thinking

The invention of the printing press by Johannes Gutenberg meant that books could be produced quickly, and knowledge could spread more rapidly. New ideas emerged, including the notion that the Earth orbits the Sun, proposed by Polish astronomer Copernicus in 1543, and Isaac Newton's theory of gravity, published in 1687.

Scientific instruments
Isaac Newton invented a new model of telescope in 1678. It used a series of mirrors to create a better-quality image.

GLOBAL AMBITIONS

Spices such as pepper and nutmeg were very expensive in Europe the 15th century, because they could only be obtained by trade w East Asia. Land routes such as the Silk Road were controlled by Islamic empires, so European explorers sought sea routes, foundi colonies and outposts in India, Southeast Asia, and the Americas.

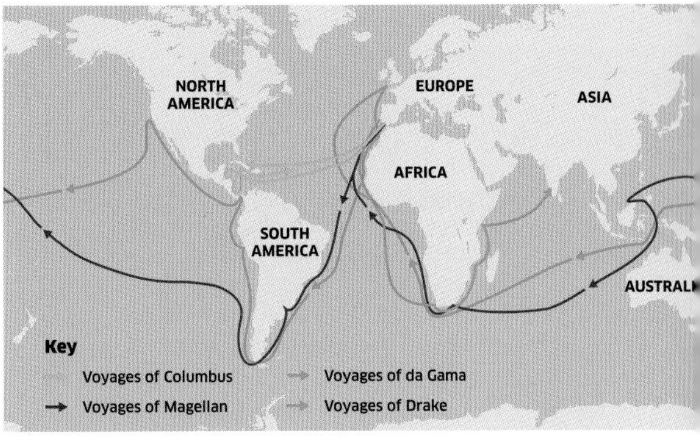

Voyages of discovery

Christopher Columbus reached America in 1492. Portuguese captain Vasco da Gama rounded southern Africa to reach India in 1498. Spaniard Ferdinand Magellan led the first voyage around the world in 1519–21, followed by Englishman Sir Francis Drake in 1577–80.

Rival explorers
Many brave explorers s out to map new sea rou and claim new territorie Some achieved great fa but many were lost at s

OF 237 MEN WHO JOINE MAGELLAN ON HIS VOYAG AROUND THE WORL **ONLY 18 RETURNED ALIV**

Trading empires

Trade with Asia and colonies in America brought great wealth t the European powers. Spanish Portuguese ships carried huge quantities of gold and silver fr the Americas, often harassed b pirates and privateers encoura by rivals such as Britain.

Vast riches
Spanish mines in the Americas produced 100 tons of silver every year–the weight of 10 buses

European powers

The influx of new wealth made some European states very powerful. Wars and rivalry were common, but the new empires also saw scientific advances and flourishing new movements in art and literature.

ELIZABETHAN ENGLAND
England grew rich during the reign of Elizabeth I (1558–1603), despite conflict between Protestants and Catholics and the threat of war with Spain.

FERDINAND AND ISABELLA OF SPAIN
The rulers of Spain, Ferdinand of Aragon and Isabella of Castile, took control of new territories in the Americas, thanks to a treaty with Portugal in 1494.

FRANCE UNDER LOUIS IV
France became the most powerful country in Europe during the long reigr of Louis XIV (1643–1715), famous for his strong army and cultured court.

RISE OF THE HABSBURGS
This family of minor nobles gained control of much of central Europe. They went on to become kings of Spain and rulers of the vast Holy Roman Empire.

THE NEW WORLD

Before the arrival of European explorers, the people of the Americas had built civilizations and empires. However, they did not have gunpowder, and even large armies could be defeated by the guns of Spanish soldiers. The Europeans also brought new diseases that killed huge numbers of indigenous Americans.

IT IS ESTIMATED THAT UP TO 90 PERCENT OF THE INDIGENOUS POPULATION OF CENTRAL AMERICA WAS WIPED OUT BY DISEASE AND WARFARE FOLLOWING THE ARRIVAL OF THE SPANISH.

Incas, Aztecs, Mayans

The most advanced peoples the Spanish encountered were the Incas (in Peru) and the Aztecs (in Mexico), both of whom controlled large empires. The Spanish attacked the Aztecs in 1519 and the Incas 1531 and soon captured their capital cities.

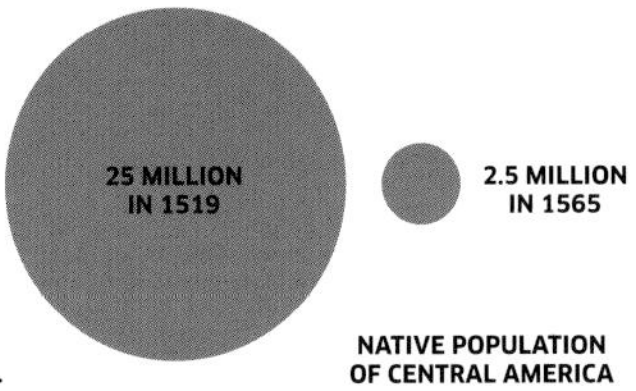

NATIVE POPULATION OF CENTRAL AMERICA

European colonies

The Spanish soon had to face competition from other European powers, who were quick to take land in the Americas. The Portuguese settled in Brazil around 1500. The French and English took islands in the Caribbean, but concentrated mainly on North America, where the English set up their first colony at Jamestown, Virginia, in 1607.

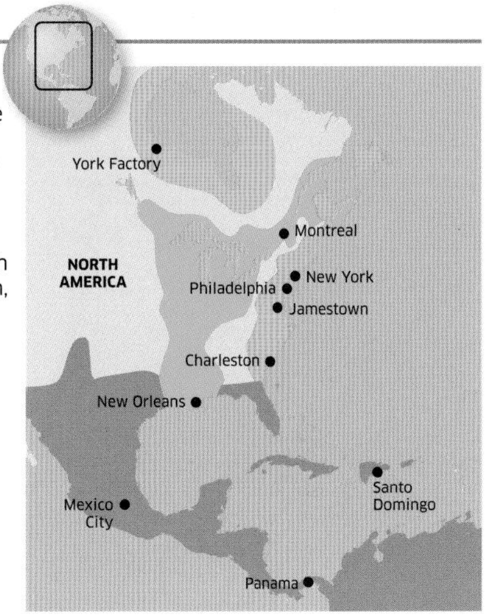

Colonial expansion
By around 1700, the Spanish controlled land as far as modern California, Texas, and Florida. North of this the French and British set up colonies.

Key
- Spanish colonies
- British colonies
- French colonies

EASTERN POWERS

In Asia, great empires continued to fight off European competition, but often suffered internal turmoil. In China, the Ming dynasty collapsed in 1644 and was replaced by the Qing, who made China strong again. Japan sealed itself off from European influence, banning foreigners for more than 200 years. Two Muslim empires, the Mughals in India and the Ottomans in Turkey, gained great power, before growing stagnant and collapsing.

Ottoman expansion

The Ottoman Empire, based in modern Turkey, quickly expanded to fill the space left by the collapse of the Byzantine Empire. They took control of the Middle East, ruling much of the Arab world. Their advance on Europe was halted by the Poles and Habsburgs on land, and in the Mediterranean by rich Italian city-states such as Venice.

SIEGE OF CONSTANTINOPLE
In 1453, the Ottoman sultan Mehmed II captured Constantinople, the capital of the Byzantine Empire. He used huge cannons to break down the strong walls. He then made the city his capital.

BATTLE OF MOHÁCS
In 1526, Sultan Süleiman the Magnificent defeated and killed the Hungarian king Louis II in a battle at Mohács. The Ottomans then took over much of Hungary. Süleiman's armies also conquered large areas of the Balkans, the Middle East, and North Africa.

BATTLE OF LEPANTO
The Ottomans captured Cyprus in 1570. A strong Spanish and Italian fleet was sent to take it back. They defeated the Turks at Lepanto, off the Greek coast, in 1571. Their victory ended Ottoman dominance in the Mediterranean.

SIEGE OF VIENNA
In 1683, an Ottoman army that had been trying to capture the Habsburg capital of Vienna (Austria) was defeated by an army led by King Jan Sobieski of Poland. The Ottomans never again reached so far west.

Qing China

In 1644, the Ming dynasty was overthrown by a series of peasant revolts. The new rulers, the Qing, came from Manchuria in northeast China. They tried to make people adopt Qing customs, like the wearing of a ponytail, but this proved very unpopular. Nevertheless, they overcame opposition and increased Chinese territory.

Greater empire
The Qing conquered new territory to make China larger than ever. The new territories included Taiwan and Mongolia.

Mughal India

In 1526, a Muslim prince from central Asia called Babur captured Delhi and founded the Mughal Empire. The Mughals expanded steadily from northern India, making their greatest gains under Sultan Akbar (1556–1605). The Mughal court was a rich one, famous for its magnificent works of art and beautiful buildings.

Combining cultures
Mughal buildings, such as the tomb of Sultan Humayun, who died in 1556, combined Islamic tradition with Indian culture to create a new style.

Tokugawa Japan

In Japan, a period of civil war ended when powerful general Tokugawa Ieyasu declared himself shogun (military ruler). He moved the capital to Edo (Tokyo) and reduced the power of the daimyo (warlords) who had previously dominated Japan. The Tokugawa family ruled Japan until 1868, and isolated it from the outside world.

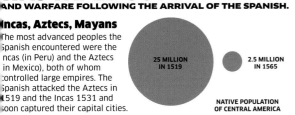

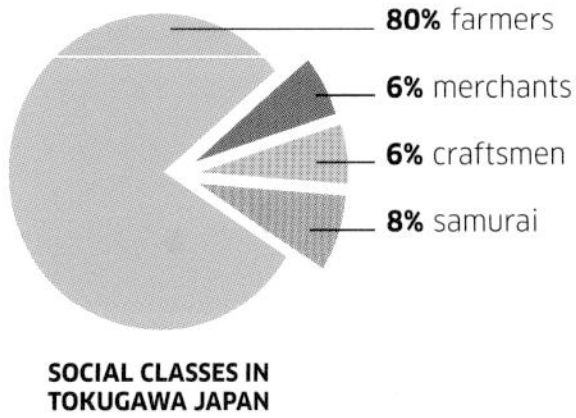

SOCIAL CLASSES IN TOKUGAWA JAPAN

Samurai society
Warrior nobles called samurai were the most honored class in Japanese society. Merchants and craftsmen may have been wealthy, but they were less respected than poor peasant farmers.

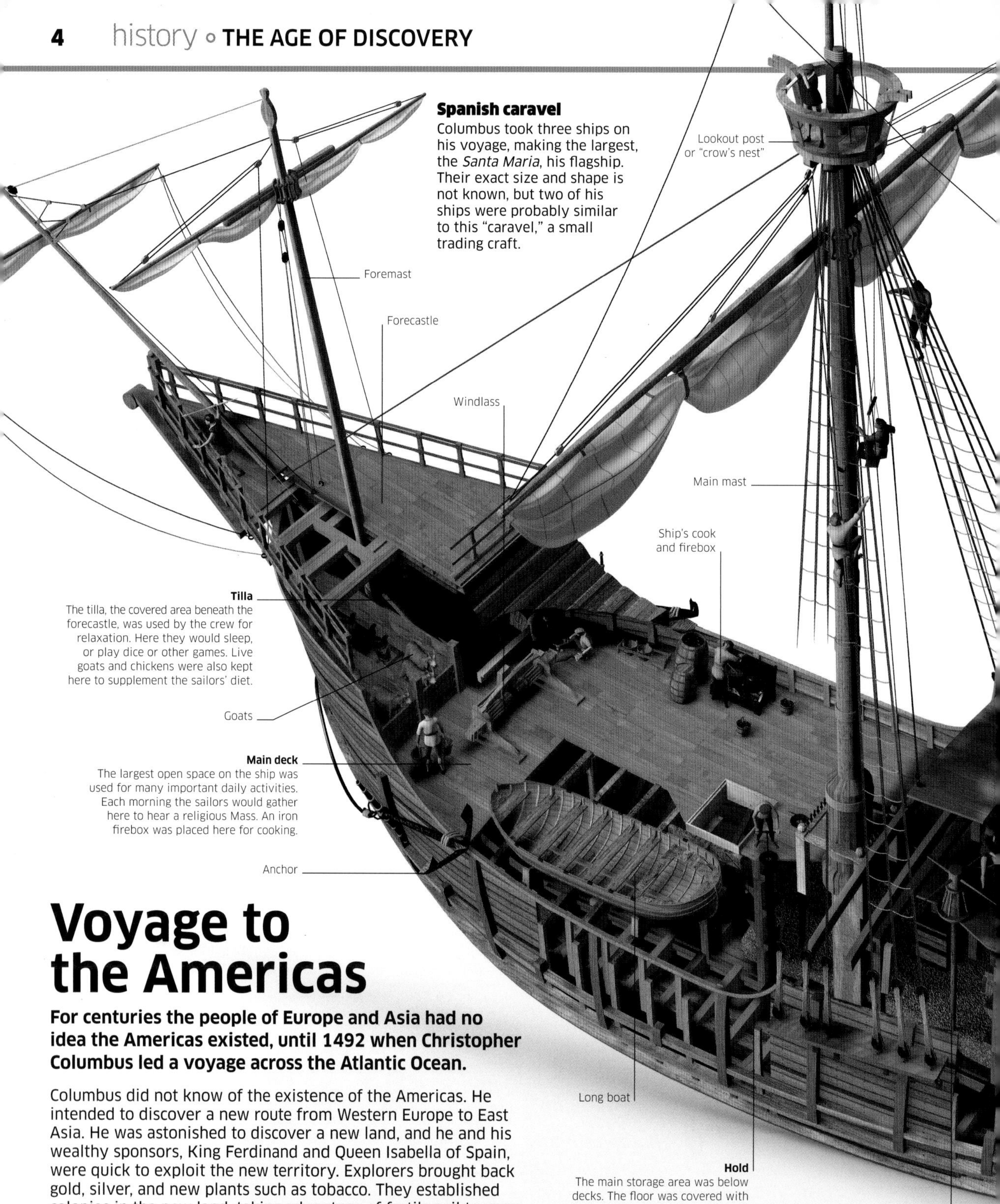

Spanish caravel
Columbus took three ships on his voyage, making the largest, the *Santa Maria*, his flagship. Their exact size and shape is not known, but two of his ships were probably similar to this "caravel," a small trading craft.
Lookout post or "crow's nest"
Foremast
Forecastle
Windlass
Main mast
Ship's cook and firebox
Tilla
The tilla, the covered area beneath the forecastle, was used by the crew for relaxation. Here they would sleep, or play dice or other games. Live goats and chickens were also kept here to supplement the sailors' diet.
Goats
Main deck
The largest open space on the ship was used for many important daily activities. Each morning the sailors would gather here to hear a religious Mass. An iron firebox was placed here for cooking.
Anchor
Long boat
Hold
The main storage area was below decks. The floor was covered with river pebbles, which kept the boat upright. The hold was filled with supplies: barrels of wine and water, beans and biscuits for food, as well as spare wood, sailcloth, and rope.
Capstan
This huge winch was pushed by eight sailors. It was used to hoist heavy loads such as supplies and the ship's anchors.

Voyage to the Americas

For centuries the people of Europe and Asia had no idea the Americas existed, until 1492 when Christopher Columbus led a voyage across the Atlantic Ocean.

Columbus did not know of the existence of the Americas. He intended to discover a new route from Western Europe to East Asia. He was astonished to discover a new land, and he and his wealthy sponsors, King Ferdinand and Queen Isabella of Spain, were quick to exploit the new territory. Explorers brought back gold, silver, and new plants such as tobacco. They established colonies in the new land, taking advantage of fertile soil to grow sugar and cotton. However, for the indigenous peoples living in the area, the arrival of European explorers was catastrophic, bringing disease, war, slavery, and death.

40 The **number of men** in the *Santa Maria's* **crew.** **70** days—the time it took **Columbus** to reach **the Americas** on his **first voyage** from Spain. **1,500** The **number of men** who joined **Columbus's second voyage.** 5

> "At two o'clock in the morning the **land was discovered,** at two leagues' distance...they found themselves near a small island, one of the Lucayos, called in the Indian language Guanahani."
> Log of Christopher Columbus, October 12, 1492

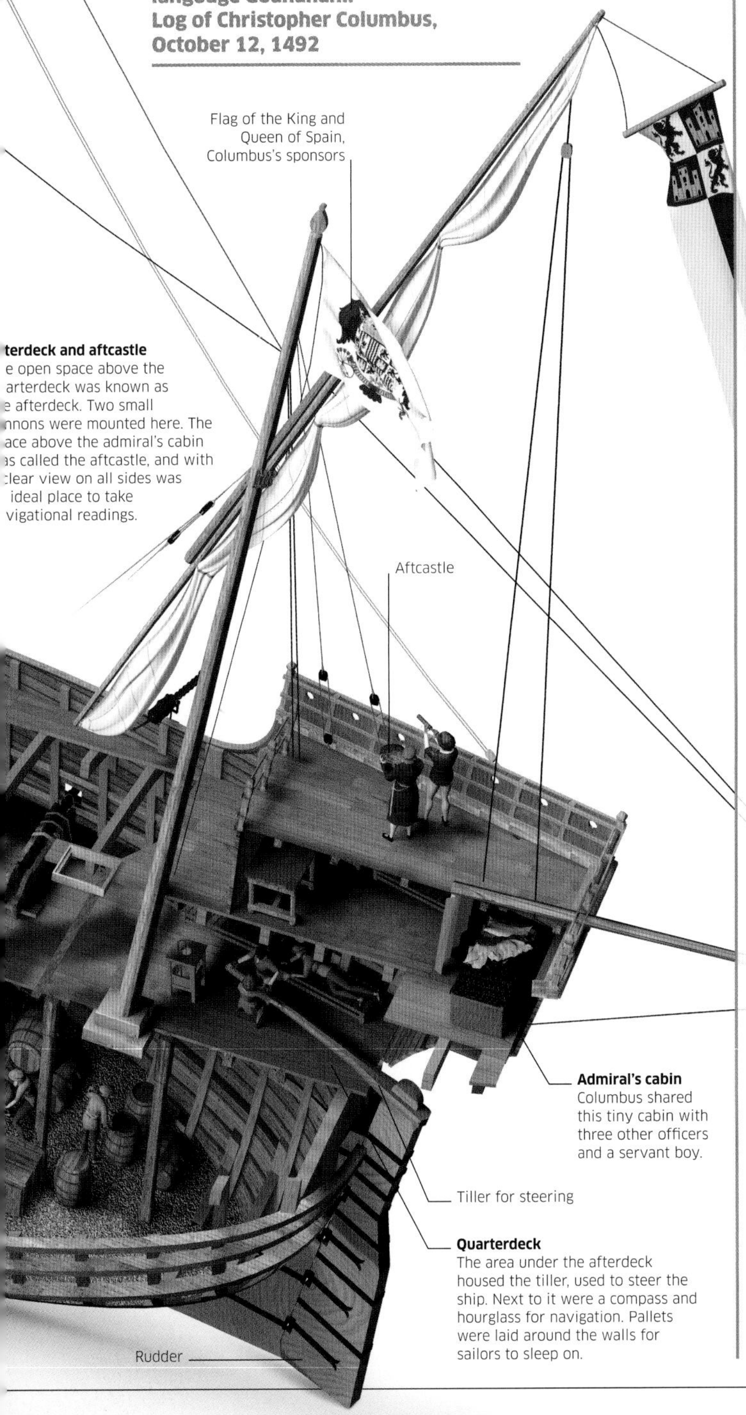

Flag of the King and Queen of Spain, Columbus's sponsors
terdeck and aftcastle
e open space above the arterdeck was known as e afterdeck. Two small nnons were mounted here. The ace above the admiral's cabin as called the aftcastle, and with clear view on all sides was ideal place to take vigational readings.
Aftcastle
Admiral's cabin
Columbus shared this tiny cabin with three other officers and a servant boy.
Tiller for steering
Quarterdeck
The area under the afterdeck housed the tiller, used to steer the ship. Next to it were a compass and hourglass for navigation. Pallets were laid around the walls for sailors to sleep on.
Rudder

Columbus's voyages

Columbus undertook four voyages to the Americas. On his first, he visited islands in the Caribbean, where his second voyage established colonies a year later. It wasn't until his third visit, in 1498, that he set foot upon the American mainland, touching the coast of what is now Venezuela. His last voyage, begun in 1502, took him along the coast of Central America, seeking a passage through to the Pacific Ocean beyond.

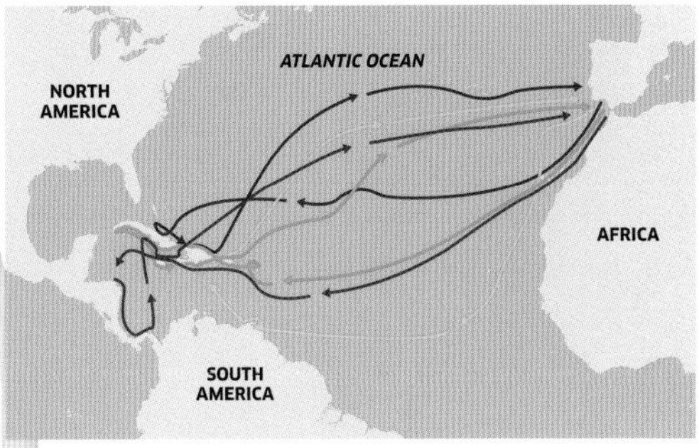

ATLANTIC OCEAN
NORTH AMERICA
AFRICA
SOUTH AMERICA

Key

- First voyage, 1492
- Second voyage, 1493
- Third voyage, 1498
- Fourth voyage, 1502

Finding your way

Explorers like Columbus often had no maps, and had to navigate by other means. They used a compass to measure the direction the ships were moving in, and an hourglass to keep track of the time. They also used a device called a quadrant, to calculate their latitude by measuring the angle of the sun and stars.

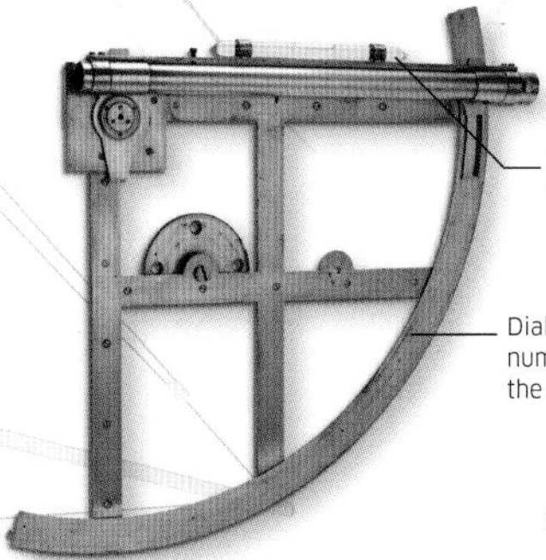

Sighting tube for aiming the quadrant
Dial marked with numbers to measure the angle of the stars

QUADRANT

COMPASS

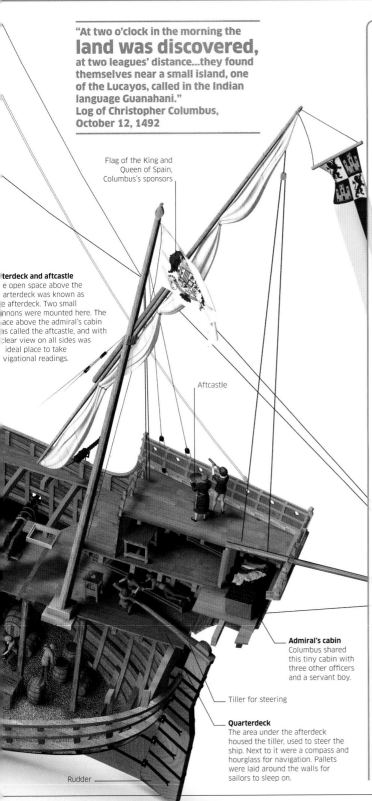

HOURGLASS

150 The number of men in the Spanish army that overthrew the Inca Emp

Human sacrifice

The Aztecs believed that the blood of human victims was needed to feed the Sun to make sure that it did not go out. Many people sacrificed to the Sun were captured in wars. The priest would plunge a sharp knife into the victim's chest and then pull out his still-beating heart.

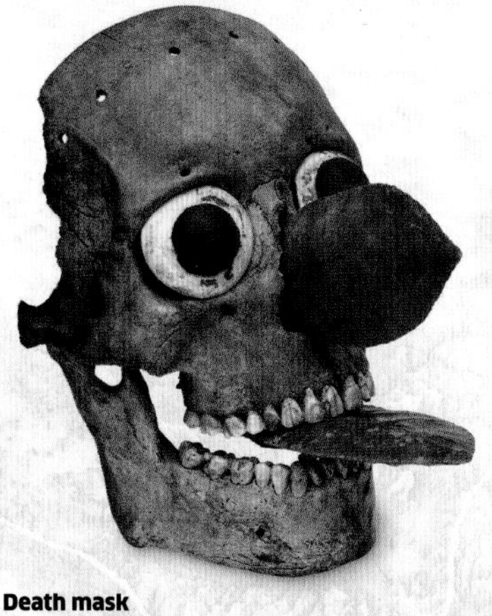

Death mask
This mask was made from the skull of a sacrificial victim and was probably worn by an Aztec priest who performed sacrifices.

The Incas

Between 1438 and 1500, the Inca people conquered a large empire in what is now Peru. Their capital was the mountain city of Qusqu. They built a road network to connect their territory, and grew rich and powerful, but the empire was destroyed by Spanish invaders in the 1530s.

Tenochtitlán
This giant Aztec city was built on an island in Lake Texcoco. Its Great Temple was dedicated to the rain god Tlaloc. The heads of sacrificial victims were hurled down its steps.

Teotihuacan
A holy site, this ancient city-state was one of the most powerful in the region, until it was destroyed and abandoned in 700 CE under mysterious circumstances.

STATUE OF TOLTEC WARRIOR

Toltecs
A warlike people, the Toltecs ruled in central Mexico before the Aztecs, from around 950 to 1150 CE. Not much is known for sure about their history, but the Aztecs are thought to have inherited aspects of their culture.

Ancient Americas

From about 3000 BCE until 1500 CE, a series of advanced cultures dominated South and Central America. Centered on powerful city-states, they were often at war with one another.

The first cities were built by the Chavín people (in South America) and the Olmecs (in Central America) in around 1000 BCE. Both of these cultures constructed huge, pyramid-shaped temples, which became a feature of the cities that were built in the region over the next 2,000 years. Different cultures rose and declined over the centuries, until most of the city-states had become part of the Inca Empire (in Peru) or the Aztec Empire (in Mexico). However, both of these empires were eventually conquered by European invaders in the early 16th century.

0,000 The population of the **Mayan city of Tikal** at its height.

500 The aproximate number of **glyphs** in the **Mayan writing system**.

1697 Date of the **conquest** of the **last Mayan city** by the Spanish.

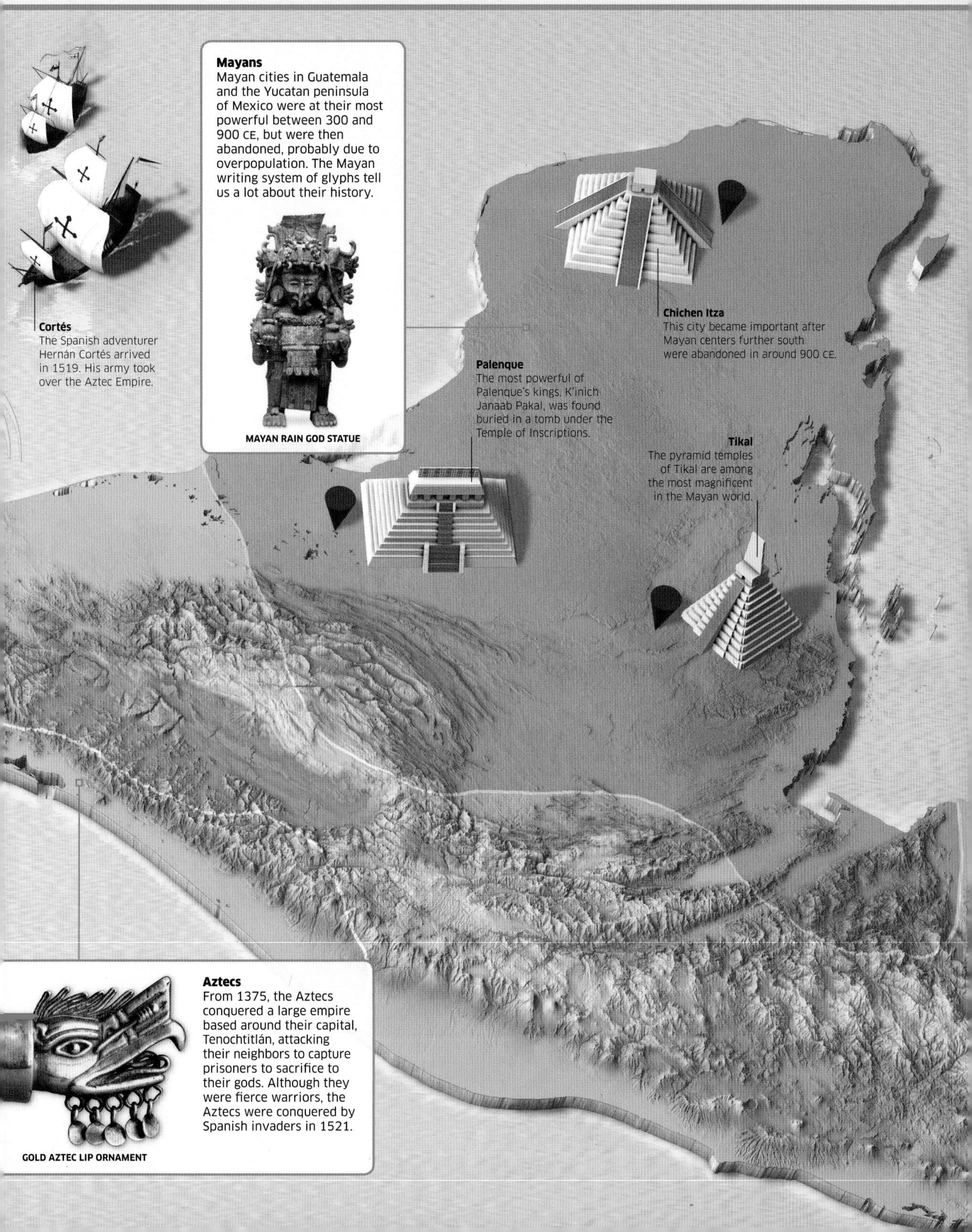

Mayans
Mayan cities in Guatemala and the Yucatan peninsula of Mexico were at their most powerful between 300 and 900 CE, but were then abandoned, probably due to overpopulation. The Mayan writing system of glyphs tell us a lot about their history.

MAYAN RAIN GOD STATUE

Cortés
The Spanish adventurer Hernán Cortés arrived in 1519. His army took over the Aztec Empire.

Chichen Itza
This city became important after Mayan centers further south were abandoned in around 900 CE.

Palenque
The most powerful of Palenque's kings, K'inich Janaab Pakal, was found buried in a tomb under the Temple of Inscriptions.

Tikal
The pyramid temples of Tikal are among the most magnificent in the Mayan world.

GOLD AZTEC LIP ORNAMENT

Aztecs
From 1375, the Aztecs conquered a large empire based around their capital, Tenochtitlán, attacking their neighbors to capture prisoners to sacrifice to their gods. Although they were fierce warriors, the Aztecs were conquered by Spanish invaders in 1521.

13,000 The approximate number of **pages of notes** left by **Leonardo da Vinci** on his death.

The Renaissance

An explosion of new ideas transformed Europe in the 15th century, bringing revolutionary works of art, science, and invention. This period has gone down in history as the Renaissance, or "rebirth."

The Renaissance began in Italy in around 1400, where scholars rediscovered the writings of Greek and Latin mathematicians, artists, and philosophers. The ideas in these texts gave rise to a school of thought called humanism, which prized experiment and experience as the sources of knowledge, in contrast to the tradition and superstition of the medieval era. This new way of thinking spread across Europe, inspiring a generation of artists, architects, and philosophers. Perhaps the most famous was Leonardo da Vinci, an ingenious scientist, artist, and inventor who represented the ideal humanist, or "Renaissance man."

New artistic techniques

One of the techniques that Renaissance scholars rediscovered was perspective—a way to give depth to paintings and drawings. Objects that are further away look smaller and shorter than objects up close. The Romans used mathematical formulas to mimic this effect in drawings. Renaissance artists copied the Roman technique to make their paintings astonishingly lifelike.

Drawing distance
Artists using perspect
show distant objects
smaller. The artist set
one or more "vanishi
points," where object
are too far away to se

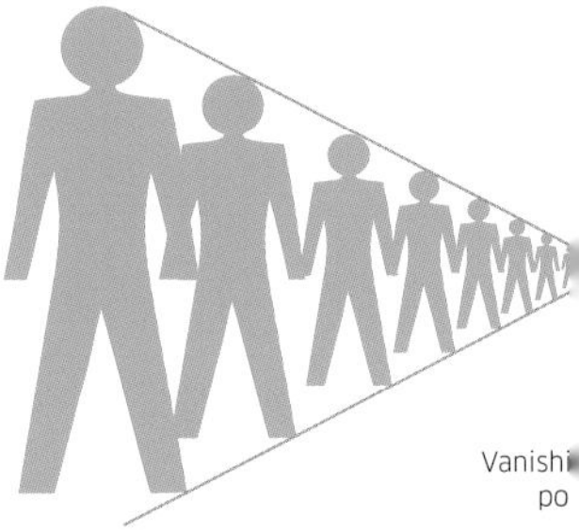

Painting

Renaissance painters tried to show their subjects as realistically as possible. They wanted their paintings to look like a window onto another scene, rather than a flat plane filled with characters. They used techniques such as perspective to give their images depth, and they painted people in a lifelike manner. They also covered a greater variety of subjects: medieval art mostly showed religious scenes and portraits, but Renaissance artists also painted scenes from history, Greek and Roman myths, and everyday life.

***The School of Athens* (1510)**
This painting was created for the Pope by Rapha
one of the most admired artists of the Renaissan
It depicts Ancient Greek philosophers, painted to
resemble Renaissance thinkers such as Leonardo
da Vinci, Michelangelo, and Raphael himself.

0 years–the time it took to build Florence Cathedral, from laying the foundations to completing the dome.

47.8 million dollars–the highest price paid for a work by a Renaissance artist (*Head of a Young Apostle* by Raphael).

9

..rchitecture

..any Italian cities contained ruins of Roman ..uildings, and the architects of the ..enaissance were determined that their ..reations should be just as grand and ..eautiful. They studied Roman writings ..n architecture and geometry to make the ..hapes of their buildings more harmonious, ..nd they copied Greek and Roman styles of ..olumns and arches for decoration.

Florence Duomo (1436)
The rulers of the city of Florence wanted their new cathedral (*duomo*) to be the envy of all their rivals. By 1413, it was almost complete, but nobody had worked out how to build its huge dome. Architect Filippo Brunelleschi solved the problem, designing a dome with two layers using lightweight bricks.

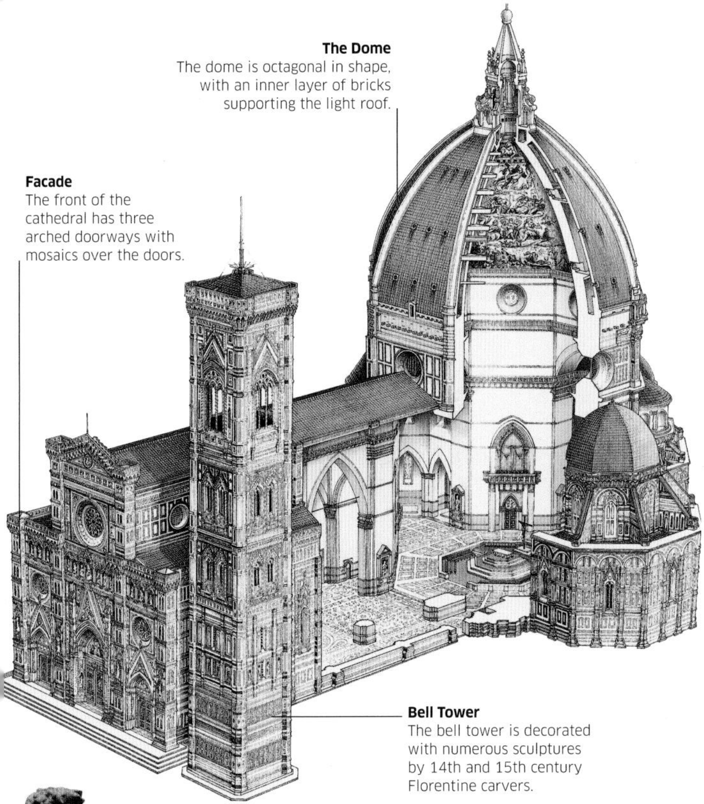

The dome is octagonal in shape, with an inner layer of bricks supporting the light roof.
Facade
The front of the cathedral has three arched doorways with mosaics over the doors.
Bell Tower
The bell tower is decorated with numerous sculptures by 14th and 15th century Florentine carvers.

Renaissance rulers

In the 15th century, Italy was made up of city-states ruled by wealthy merchant families. Their dukes and princes acted as patrons, paying for artists and thinkers to create artworks, monuments, and inventions to impress rival rulers. New political ideas arose. These were most famously summed up by a diplomat named Niccolò Machiavelli, who advised nobles to be unjust or even cruel in order to achieve noble ends.

Medici coat of arms
The Medici family ruled Florence from 1434. The balls on their coat of arms may represent coins, showing their origins as traders and bankers.

"MEN ARE DRIVEN BY TWO IMPULSES,
LOVE AND FEAR... IT IS MUCH SAFER TO BE FEARED THAN LOVED."
NICCOLÒ MACHIAVELLI, *THE PRINCE*, 1513

The Northern Renaissance

From Italy, the ideas of the Renaissance quickly spread to Northern Europe. Rich kings such as Francis I of France and wealthy merchants in Belgium and the Netherlands, were eager to benefit from the new ideas. Their artists followed the techniques of the Italian Renaissance, and developed new styles of their own. Scholars such as Dutchman Desiderius Erasmus translated Greek and Roman texts into versions that could be widely read.

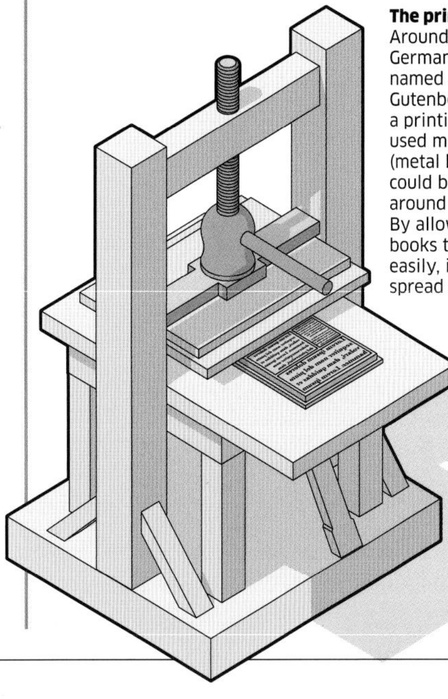

The printing press
Around1455, a German blacksmith named Johannes Gutenberg invented a printing press that used movable type (metal letters that could be swapped around and reused). By allowing copies of books to be printed easily, it sped up the spread of ideas.

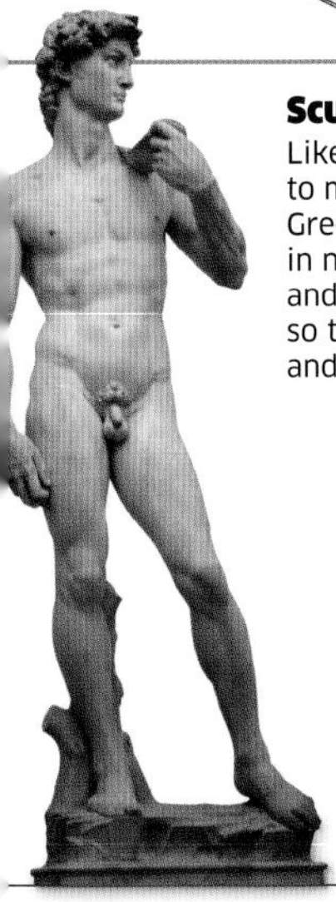

Sculpture

Like the painters of the era, Renaissance sculptors tried to make their works as lifelike as possible. Inspired by Greek and Roman sculptures, they showed their subjects in natural poses, and brought out details such as hairs and folds of cloth. Many artists studied human anatomy so that their works copied the shapes of limbs, muscles, and veins exactly as they appear in real life.

Renaissance doctors and artists studied human anatomy by dissecting (cutting open) the bodies of dead criminals.

Michelangelo's *David* (1504)
Michelangelo was one of the greatest painters and sculptors of the Renaissance. His sculpture of David, biblical King of Israel, is regarded as one of the most perfect human figures ever carved in marble.

40,000 The approximate number of characters used to write in traditional Chinese.

The Great Wall

For centuries, China's greatest threat came from the north, where warlike tribes mounted swift, fierce raids on unprotected settlements. To keep them out, the Chinese emperors built a series of walls stretching thousands of miles.

Signal tower
Often built on high points to be easily seen, these towers were used to send signals along the wall.
Signal cannon
The noise of the cannon could be used to signal at night, when smoke could not be seen.
Brazier for sending smoke signals
Garrison
Small numbers of troops were stationed at regular intervals along the wall to watch for invaders.
Bamboo supports
Rubble filling
The inside of the wall was filled with broken stones and mud.
Stone layers
The outsides of the wall were built of stone and fired bricks.

5 ft (7.5 m)—the **thickness** of the **wall** at its **widest**.

13,170 miles (21,196 km)—the **length** of the **Great Wall**.

9,999 Said to be the **number of rooms** in the **Forbidden City**.

11

mperial China

**its height, China was the most powerful empire in
: world. Its emperors controlled wealth and influence
yond the wildest dreams of European monarchs.**

na is one of the world's oldest civilizations, with written records ng back almost 3,500 years. Its history includes long periods of l war and conflict with its neighbors. Despite all this, Chinese berial society was generally extremely stable and well organized. m the 1st century BCE, the government was run by a civil service, ich later on could only be entered by passing difficult exams. Chinese lorers established trade routes as far as Africa and Arabia, and nese craftsmen created some of the most important inventions uman history, including paper, gunpowder, and porcelain.

The path of the wall
The earliest parts of the wall were built in the 7th century BCE, to protect Chinese farmland from nomadic raiders to the north. They were first joined together in the 3rd century BCE under Qin Shi Huangdi. Successive Chinese emperors fortified and extended these walls, and they reached their greatest extent in the 16th century, under the rule of the Ming emperors.

Imperial families

Several different dynasties rose to power over the centuries. Some brought war and famine, while others saw incredible advances in philosophy, technology, and art. The first ruling dynasty began in the 16th century BCE under the Shang, but they controlled only a part of the vast empire that would follow.

1050–256 BCE

Zhou dynasty

The Zhou conquered their neighbors to build an empire across China. Great sages lived under their rule: Laozi, founder of Tao philosophy, and Kong Fuzi (Confucius), whose code still influences Chinese culture today.

CHARIOT DECORATION

475–221 BCE

Warring States period

Rival states formed after the decline of the Zhou. Their rulers fought for land and power, using strict military organization to raise and control their armies.

LEATHER ARMOR

221 BCE

China united

The Warring States period ended with victory by the Qin kingdom, reuniting China after centuries of war. Qin Shi Huangdi became emperor. He built new roads and canals, and introduced consistent weights and measures across the empire.

210 BCE

Death of an emperor

Qin Shi Huangdi died 11 years after becoming emperor. He was buried in a vast tomb complex guarded by an army of thousands of terra-cotta warriors, complete with weapons and armor.

206 BCE – 220 CE

Han dynasty

Qin Shi Huangdi's son ruled for only four years, and died during a popular rebellion. Liu Bang, a peasant who had risen to become a powerful general, took control of the empire, founding the Han dynasty.

HAN LACQUER BOWL

618–1279

Tang and Song dynasties

After centuries of turmoil, China returned to peace under the Tang and Song dynasties. Art, literature, and invention flourished as the empire expanded and China became very wealthy.

TANG MODEL HORSE

1368–1644

Ming dynasty

After the fall of the Song, China was ruled by Mongols from the north for many years. They were overthrown by rebel Zhu Yuanzhang. His descendants, the Ming emperors, ruled from a huge palace called the Forbidden City.

MING VASE

1912

The last emperor

By the 19th century, China had come into conflict with European powers. The emperors were weakened and, in 1912, a military revolt deposed the Qing rulers and founded the Republic of China.

13 The age at which Akbar took the throne.

Rulers of India

The Mughals were warrior horsemen from Central Asia who swept through northern India in the 16th century. Their rulers built a great empire in which Hindu and Muslim people lived side by side in relative peace.

The Mughals invaded India in 1526 under the command of the warrior Babur. They captured the important northern Indian city of Delhi, and Babur became the first Mughal emperor. Within 150 years, his descendants had expanded their empire to include most of India.

The Mughals ruled over 150 million people. A Muslim people, they were tolerant toward the religion of their Hindu subjects. The emperors were lavish patrons of the arts, and their craftsmen built many beautiful buildings. Yet only a century after reaching the height of its power, the Mughal Empire had lost most of its territory.

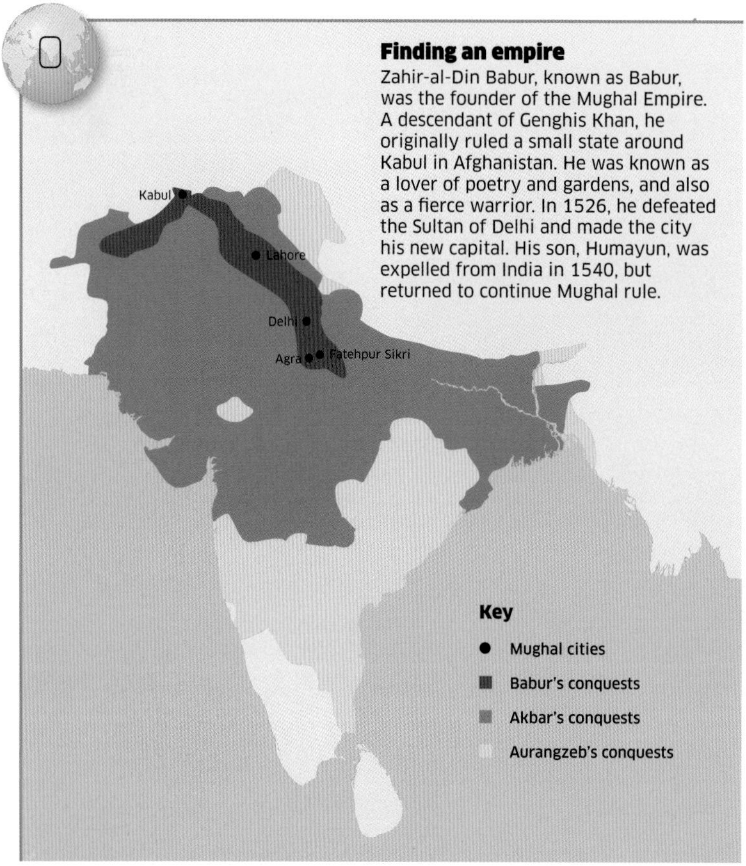

Finding an empire

Zahir-al-Din Babur, known as Babur, was the founder of the Mughal Empire. A descendant of Genghis Khan, he originally ruled a small state around Kabul in Afghanistan. He was known as a lover of poetry and gardens, and also as a fierce warrior. In 1526, he defeated the Sultan of Delhi and made the city his new capital. His son, Humayun, was expelled from India in 1540, but returned to continue Mughal rule.

Arms and armor

Mughal warriors mostly fought on horseback. They wore chain mail over their lower neck, arms, body, and upper legs, with an iron breastplate for extra protection. Their armies were also well equipped with guns and cannons.

Battle and conquest

The Mughal Empire was founded after a great battle at Panipat near Delhi in April 1526, where Babur's army of just 12,000 defeated an enemy force of 100,000 me[n] and 1,000 elephants. Babur's men had the advantage o[f] gunpowder weapons (cannons and handguns), which th[eir] opponents lacked. The Mughal army went on to conque[r] other Indian kingdoms, and absorbed their warriors int[o] its ranks, gaining well-trained heavy cavalry and eventually amassing 100,000 men.

Mughal lords

From the mid-16th century, the Mughal Empire entered a golden age during which its rulers established a strong government and conquered new territories. They grew wealthy and powerful, leaving behind great monuments, many of which survive to this day.

Akbar "The Great" (1556–1605)

The third emperor, Akbar, is considered one of the greatest rulers of all time. He was fierce to his enemies, defeating the Afghans and Uzbeks, and conquering Gujarat and Bengal. But he was wise and gentle with his subjects, allying with the Hindu Rajput kings, who joined his empire, and promoting peace and religious tolerance across the empire.

Jahangir (1605–27)

Akbar's son, Jahangir, focused more on managing the empire than conquering new territory. But he did defeat the last of the Rajputs who had refused his father's alliance. Jahangir was a great patron of the arts. During his reign, Mughal painters developed an exquisite new style based on carefully recording the world around them.

Shah Jahan (1627–58)

Shah Jahan, who had rebelled against his father, Jahangir, took the throne on h[is] father's death. He expanded the Mughal Empire further and built a new city, Shahjahanabad, as his capital. Shah Jaha[n] was an active patron of religion and the arts. Mughal architecture flourished unde[r] his rule, and he ordered the Taj Mahal built as a mausoleum for his wife.

square miles (15 km²)—the area of Akbar's capital at Fatehpur Sikri.

86 The number of tigers killed by Jahangir while hunting.

141,053 The number of war elephants in the Mughal emperors' army.

13

he end of the empire

nah Jahan's son, Aurangzeb, conquered new rovinces in the south of India, expanding Mughal erritory by a quarter. But the empire came under ttack from a new power, the Maratha Confederacy. onstant wars drained the Mughal treasury and ne empire began to crumble. Aurangzeb was also npopular with Hindus and other non-Muslim ubjects. After he died in 1707, the empire fell part, with weak rulers unable to defend it from s enemies. In 1739, the Persian ruler Nadir Shah nvaded, sacking the city of Delhi and carrying off nany Mughal treasures. By 1857, the Mughals ruled nly central Delhi. Emperor Bahahdur Shah joined rebellion against the British in 1857. He was eposed and the Mughal Empire came to an end.

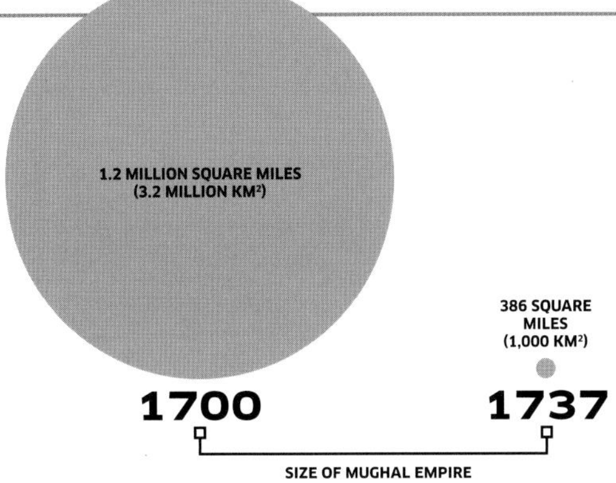

1.2 MILLION SQUARE MILES (3.2 MILLION KM²)
386 SQUARE MILES (1,000 KM²)
1700
1737
SIZE OF MUGHAL EMPIRE

27 years—the length of the war between the Maratha Confederacy and the Mughal Empire.

lughal art

rt and architecture flourished under the Mughals. lanuscripts with delicate paintings were especially prized. hese now provide us with lots of information about the lughal court. The emperors ordered new cities full of vonderful buildings to be constructed, such as Fatehpur ikri and Shahjahanabad. Some of their buildings, such as the Taj Mahal at Agra, are world famous to this day.

The Taj Mahal

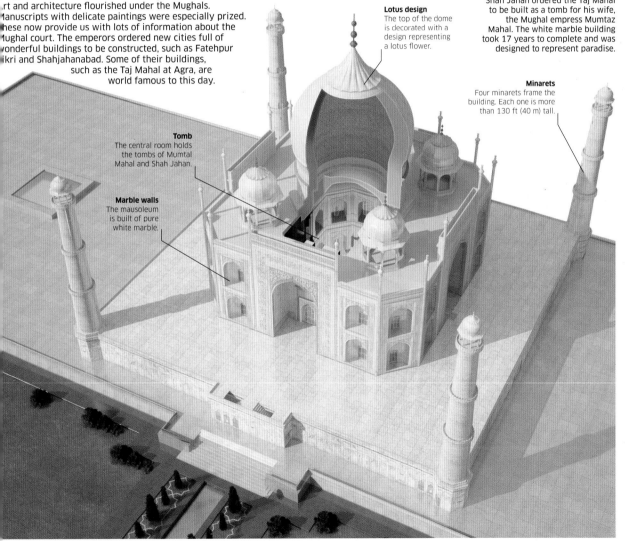

Shah Jahan ordered the Taj Mahal to be built as a tomb for his wife, the Mughal empress Mumtaz Mahal. The white marble building took 17 years to complete and was designed to represent paradise.

The central room holds the tombs of Mumtal Mahal and Shah Jahan.
Marble walls
The mausoleum is built of pure white marble.

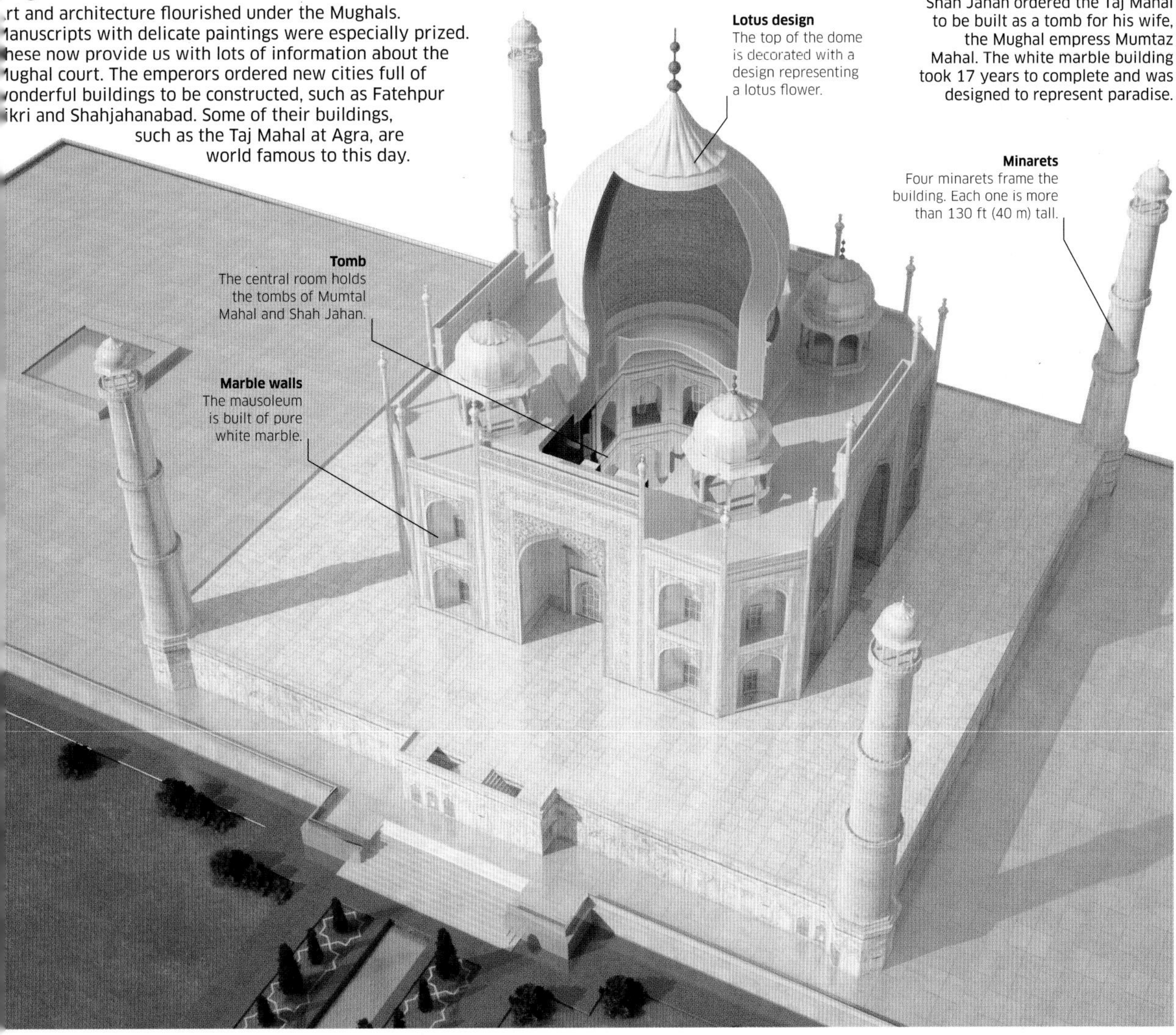

Lotus design
The top of the dome is decorated with a design representing a lotus flower.
Minarets
Four minarets frame the building. Each one is more than 130 ft (40 m) tall.

THE MODERN WORLD

The years since 1750 have seen huge turbulence in every area of life. Globe-spanning empires arose in the 19th century, and fell apart as the balance of power shifted from nobles and emperors to everyday citizens. New technology transformed agriculture, industry, transport, and warfare, and a digital revolution changed communications and entertainment forever.

THE AGE OF REVOLUTION

From around 1750, new political movements called for kings and governments to grant more freedom to the people. At the same time, colonies began to seek independence from their ruling countries. When rulers and colonial powers refused these demands, the populace rose up in rebellion. The USA won their independence from Britain by force in 1783, inspiring other revolutions.

The French Revolution

In 1789, the French people rebelled. King Louis XVI was deposed and executed. The Revolution became a bloodbath, as the new leaders turned on each other in an era of violence known as the Terror.

Napoleon Bonparte
After the French Revolution, a popular general named Napoleon became Emperor of France, and began a long and bloody war of conquest across Europe.

Liberation in Latin America

Between 1813 and 1822, revolutionary movements led by Simón Bolivar and José de San Martin freed most of South America from Spanish control. Mexico, too, became independent after a revolution headed by Miguel Hidalgo.

The arrival of communism

In the 19th century, German philosopher Karl Marx proposed a new theory of government called communism. It argued that the wealth of a country should be shared equally among all its citizens. In 1917, revolutionaries in Russia overthrew the emperor (or tsar) to establish the world's first communist state. It would go on to become the USSR, one of the superpowers of the 20th century.

Vladimir Lenin
After the overthrow of the tsar, Lenin declared himself leader of the people. He was the head of the communist government until his death in 1924.

AGE OF IMPERIALISM

During the 19th century, European countries expanded their overseas colonies into vast empires. European armies were well trained and armed with guns, and were easily able to overcome resistance to their expansion. This policy of acquiring new coloni known as imperialism, spread European rule over much of Africa Australasia, and large parts of Asia by 1900.

Dividing the world

By 1914, a few powerful countries had control over almost every part of the world. The largest empire belonged to the British. Their colonies were guarded by a powerful navy, which controlled seas and oceans around the world.

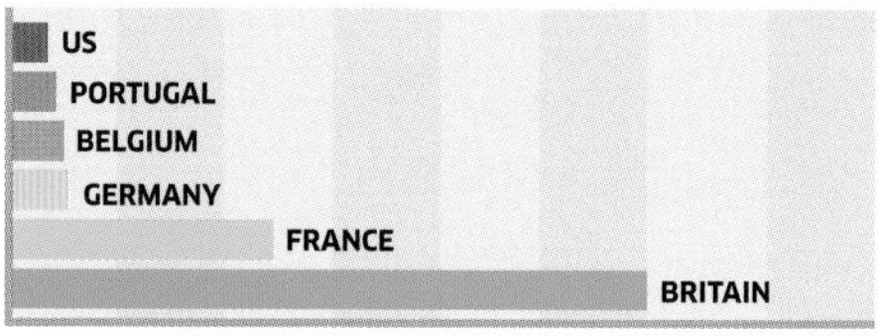

RELATIVE SIZE OF EMPIRES

Imperial land
By 1910, Britai was well ahead the imperial rac with an empire covering more than twice as m of the globe as closest rival, Fr

RELATIVE COLONIAL POPULATIONS

Imperial popula
Millions of peop across the worl lived under colc rule by 1910. Britian governe subjects in Afric the Americas, A and Australasia

Imperial rivals

Wars in this period became ever larger and more bloody as rival empires threw their full might against each other.

- **Seven Years War (1756–63)**
  The world's first global war was fought mainly between the empires of Britain and France over colonies in India and North America.
- **Napoleonic Wars (1803–15)**
  Napoleon Bonaparte proclaimed himself Emperor of France and waged a war of conquest, but was defeated at Waterloo by an alliance of European powers.
- **Crimean War (1853–56)**
  Russia's attempts to capture land from the Ottoman Empire were halted when Britain and France allied against them.
- **Opium wars (1839–60)**
  The Chinese tried to stop British merchants from trading in opium, sparking two wars with Britain. The fighting ended with the Chinese forced to open 14 ports to European trade.
- **Russo-Japanese War (1904–05)**
  Japan's powerful, modernized army and navy inflicted a shock defeat on Russia in a war over territory in China and Korea.

A postcolonial world

European colonies in Asia and Africa found it harder to win independence than those in America. However, two World W greatly weakened the European empires. India and Pakistan wor their independence from Britair 1947, after mass popular protes led by a lawyer named Gandhi. Africa, Ghana was the first colo to win independence in 1957, a many others soon followed.

"YOU CA
CHAIN ME
YOU CAN TORTURE M
YOU CAN EVE
DESTRO
THIS BOD
BUT YO
WILL NEVE
IMPRISO
MY MIND
GANDHI, CAMPAIGNER
INDIAN INDEPENDE

A CENTURY OF CONFLICT

he first half of the 20th century saw wo of the bloodiest wars in human istory. Each started with conflicts in urope, then spread to countries all cross the world. World War I 1914–18) saw millions of fighting nen killed in bitter trench warfare. Vorld War II (1939–45) brought attles between armies of tanks and ircraft, and the development of the tomic bomb. When the dust had ettled, the world's most powerful ations were the US and the ommunist USSR. They fought a Cold Var, backed by vast nuclear arsenals.

World War I

In 1914, the killing of Archduke Franz Ferdinand of Austria in Sarajevo caused a war between the German-led Central Powers and the Allies (led by the French and British). Much of the fighting happened on the Western Front in France and Belgium, where attempts to capture heavily defended trench systems caused massive casualties. Only in 1918 did the Allies break through and defeat Germany.

World War I cemetery
Nearly 10 million soldiers died during World War I. Many of them were buried in graveyards near where they fell.

World War II

In 1933, Adolf Hitler became leader of Germany. His campaign to conquer neighboring countries set off a new global conflict in 1939. German armies were victorious at first, but were defeated in 1945 by their Allied enemies. Japan joined the war in 1941, but was forced to surrender after the US attacked with atomic bombs in 1945.

A terrible cost
World War II caused between 60 and 80 million deaths, estimated to be around 4 percent of the entire population of the world before the war.

he Cold War

lthough the US and USSR had een allies in World War II, they ecame enemies once it was over. hey did not fight directly, but ought a "Cold War" by other neans, such as overthrowing overnments friendly to the other ide. The Cold War was especially angerous since both sides had uclear weapons that could have illed many millions of people.

IN 1982, THE USSR AND US BETWEEN THEM HAD MORE THAN 20,000 NUCLEAR WARHEADS **WITH A COMBINED EXPLOSIVE POWER ESTIMATED** AT MORE THAN 12,000 MEGATONS, OR 1 MILLION TIMES THE ENERGY **RELEASED BY THE BOMB THAT DESTROYED HIROSHIMA.**

A TRANSFORMED WORLD

Vhile wars and revolutions brought political changes, dvances in science and technology transformed society. Developments in medicine created cures for diseases hat had killed millions. The Industrial Revolution rought new machines that could do the work of dozens f workers. These new societies brought much greater quality, and the old order was overturned, as women nd nonwhite people fought to win equal rights.

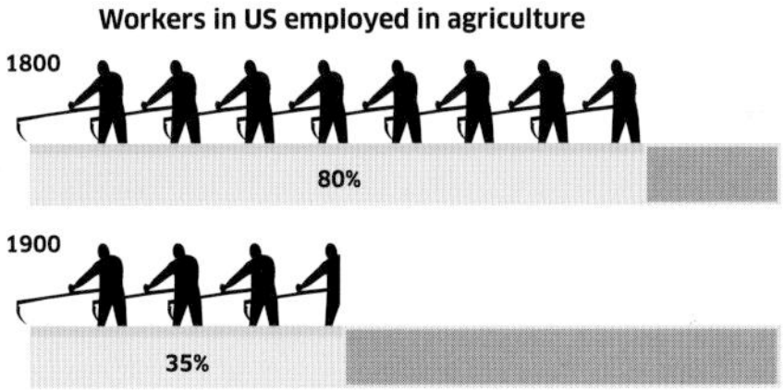

The rise of industry

The Industrial Revolution brought great new advances, but also new problems. Goods and household items became cheaper as they were mass-produced in factories instead of being made by hand. However, many workers were badly paid and lived in terrible poverty, especially in cities.

qual rights

efore the 20th century, women, frican-Americans, and nonwhites n European colonies were often enied basic freedoms. It took the etermination of many brave ampaigners to ensure that basic ights such as voting and education vere available to all.

- **1893** New Zealand becomes first country to grant women the right to vote in national elections.
- **1920** 19th Amendment to the United States Constitution grants women the vote.
- **1948** South Africa begins passing legislation discriminating against nonwhites. This policy is called apartheid.
- **1964** The Civil Rights Act makes it illegal in the USA to deny black people equal access to education and housing.
- **1965** Voting Rights Act (US) removes obstacles to African-Americans voting.
- **1994** South Africa holds first elections in which adults of all racial groups can vote, ending apartheid.

ence and medicines

he 20th century saw scientific advances beyond anything in uman history. Antibiotics cured untreatable diseases, and cars nd airplanes reduced journeys that would have taken days or veeks to a few hours. Human beings discovered ever more bout the universe, their history, and themselves.

"ANYONE WHO HAS NEVER MADE A MISTAKE HAS NEVER TRIED **ANYTHING NEW."**
ALBERT EINSTEIN

Environmental challenges

The 19th and 20th centuries saw a rapid rise in the world's population, and a huge increase in the resources human beings use. Supplies such as coal, oil, and even fresh water may become scarce. Many natural habitats have been damaged by pollution or human exploitation. Rising global temperatures threaten to disrupt vast areas of farmland and human living space across the world.

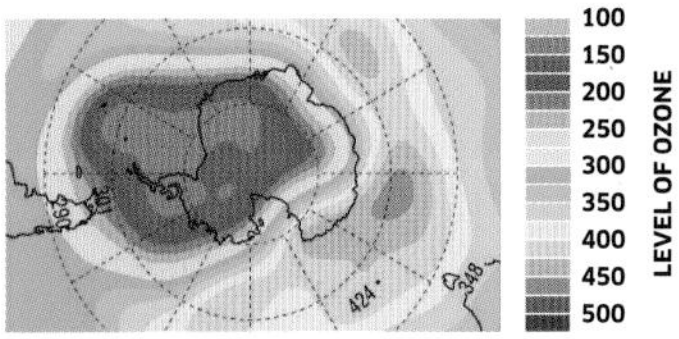

Ozone hole
In the 1990s, air pollution led to a breakdown in the ozone layer, a part of the atmosphere that protects the Earth from harmful radiation. At its biggest, the hole, situated above Antarctica, was twice the area of Europe.

115 The number of **gallons of rum** that could be **exchanged for a male slave** in 1756.

North America
Around 650,000 African slaves were taken to plantations in what is now the southern US. In the north, which was more industrial, merchants sometimes took the place of Europe in the triangular slave trade, selling manufactured goods directly to Africa in exchange for slaves. The international slave trade was banned by the US in 1808.

IRON TO BRAND SLAVES

Slave plantations
Most slaves transported to the Americas were brought to work on cotton, sugar, and tobacco plantations in the Caribbean, southern US, and Brazil. Conditions were harsh—the slaves were often branded or shackled, and overseers, those who organized the work on the plantations, were cruel.

The slave trade

European settlers in America needed laborers to work on plantations. Between 1500 and 1900, this led to 12 million African slaves being taken to the Americas.

The slave trade is often called the "Triangular Trade" because it had three stages. Goods from Europe were traded in Africa for slaves, who crossed the Atlantic in a journey known as the Middle Passage. These slaves were then exchanged for crops to be sold in Europe. Many slaves died on the journey to the Americas, and those who survived faced appalling working conditions on the plantations. An international campaign banned the Atlantic slave trade in the 19th century.

39 The **percentage of slaves** carried on the Middle Passage who **went to Brazil**.

4 million—the estimated **number of slaves in the US** at the time of **abolition in 1865.**

17

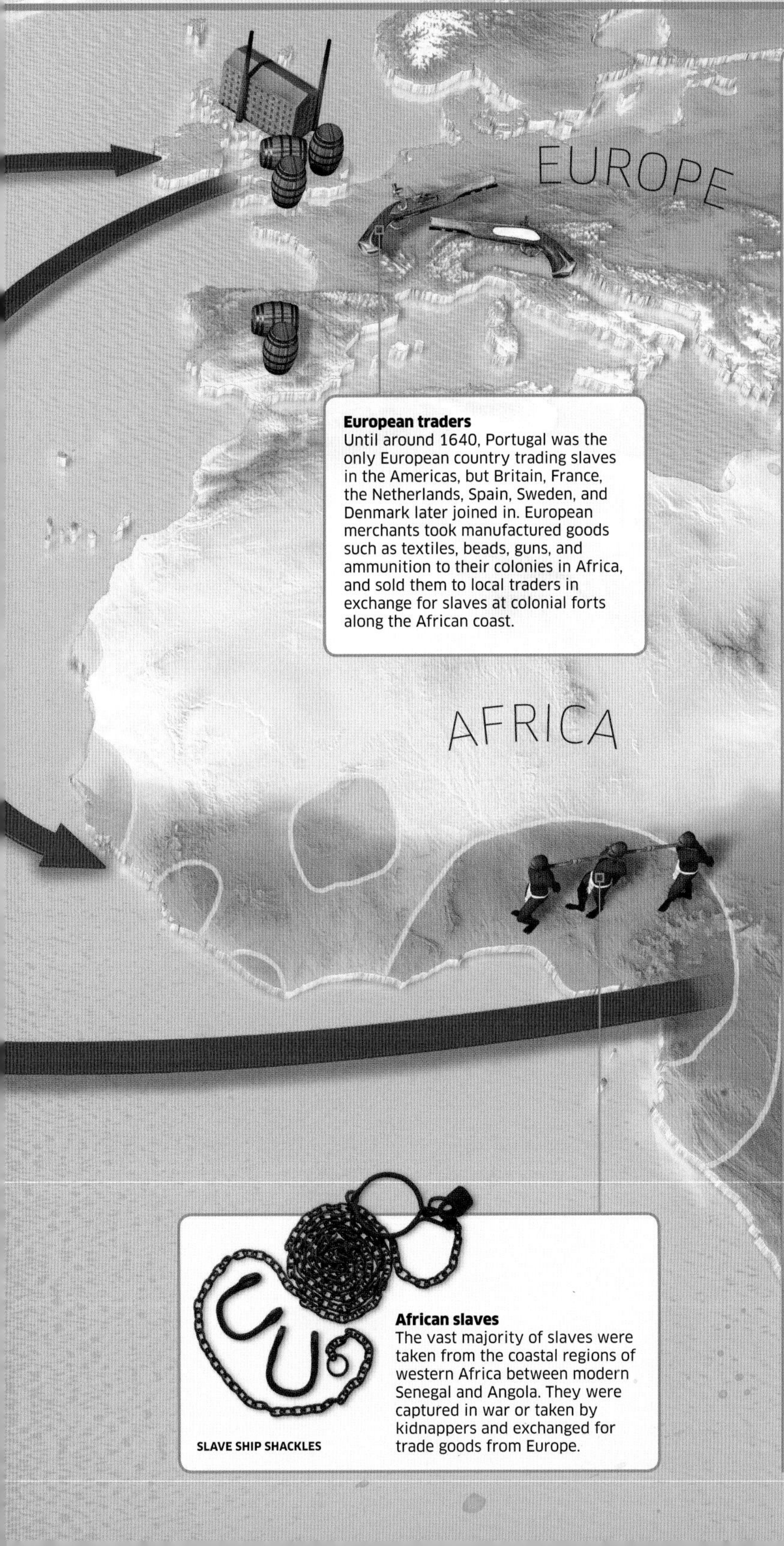

European traders
Until around 1640, Portugal was the only European country trading slaves in the Americas, but Britain, France, the Netherlands, Spain, Sweden, and Denmark later joined in. European merchants took manufactured goods such as textiles, beads, guns, and ammunition to their colonies in Africa, and sold them to local traders in exchange for slaves at colonial forts along the African coast.

SLAVE SHIP SHACKLES

African slaves
The vast majority of slaves were taken from the coastal regions of western Africa between modern Senegal and Angola. They were captured in war or taken by kidnappers and exchanged for trade goods from Europe.

Terrible conditions

On the voyage across the Atlantic, which could last from six weeks to six months, slaves were crammed together below deck in the ship's hold, with little fresh food or water. Male slaves were chained together to prevent them from attacking the crew.

Slave ship
To make the most profit possible, the traders packed slaves into very small spaces, sometimes less than 12 in (30 cm) high. One infamous slave ship, the *Brooke*, carried as many as 600 slaves, shackled together in pairs.

"THE NUMBER IN THE SHIP, **WHICH WAS SO CROWDED** THAT EACH HAD **SCARCELY ROOM** TO TURN HIMSELF, ALMOST **SUFFOCATED US."**
OLAUDAH EQUIANO
(FORMER SLAVE)

A deadly voyage

Cramped conditions and lack of food and water meant that 1.8 million slaves died of disease or starvation while voyaging to the Americas on the Middle Passage. Their bodies were thrown overboard.

Death toll
The death rate for slaves reached as high as one in four on the worst Atlantic voyages.

Calling for an end

Calls to put an end to the inhumanity of the slave trade led to its abolition in Britain in 1807. Other countries soon followed, until the final country to end the trade, Brazil, did so in 1831.

"NEVER, NEVER WILL WE DESIST TILL WE HAVE WIPED **AWAY THIS SCANDAL FROM THE CHRISTIAN NAME,** RELEASED OURSELVES FROM THE LOAD OF GUILT, UNDER WHICH **WE AT PRESENT LABOR,** AND EXTINGUISHED EVERY TRACE **OF THIS BLOODY TRAFFIC."**
WILLIAM WILBERFORCE
(ANTISLAVERY CAMPAIGNER)

72,000 The approximate number of articles in Diderot's *Encyclopédie.*

The Enlightenment

The 18th century was a time of revolution. The power of governments, religious beliefs, and scientific principles were all challenged by a wave of new thinkers determined to replace outdated traditions.

The Renaissance had brought new ways of thinking about science and philosophy, but they were still based on old traditions: the teachings of the Church and writings of the Ancient Greeks and Romans. The thinkers of the Enlightenment wanted to replace these sources of wisdom with individual observation, experiment, and logic—the rule of reason. Their radical ideas would bring wars, revolutions, and the beginnings of modern science.

Revolution of ideas

In the 18th century, people who wanted to know about the world studied natural philosophy, which included all the sciences and maths. At the time, a flood of new information was spreading across Europe, helped by new discoveries of explorers in Asia, Africa, and the Americas, and by the printing press. A group of natural philosophers in Paris, led by Denis Diderot and Jean d'Alembert, compiled an *Encyclopédie*, a giant, 28-volume work summing up everything they knew about art, science, and crafts. Their message was that reason and science could be applied to almost any subject, and their ideas spread across Europe and America. German philosopher Immanuel Kant summed up the new way of thinking as: "Dare to know. Have courage to use your own understanding."

The *Encyclopédie*
Diderot's great work covered not only art and science but everyday professions, such as music, cooking, and even farming.

Isaac Newton

One of the founding figures of the Enlightenment was the English scientist Isaac Newton (1642–1727). He is most famous for working out the laws of gravity and motion, which showed how the movements of the Moon and stars follow the same laws as the movements of objects on Earth. He also made vital discoveries about the nature of light and heat, and was one of the first to formulate a mathematical process called calculus. His curiosity about th world sometimes led him to dc strange things. For example, he pushed a blunt needle into his eye socket to see how changin the shape of his eyeball affect his vision, as part of his studie into how light moves.

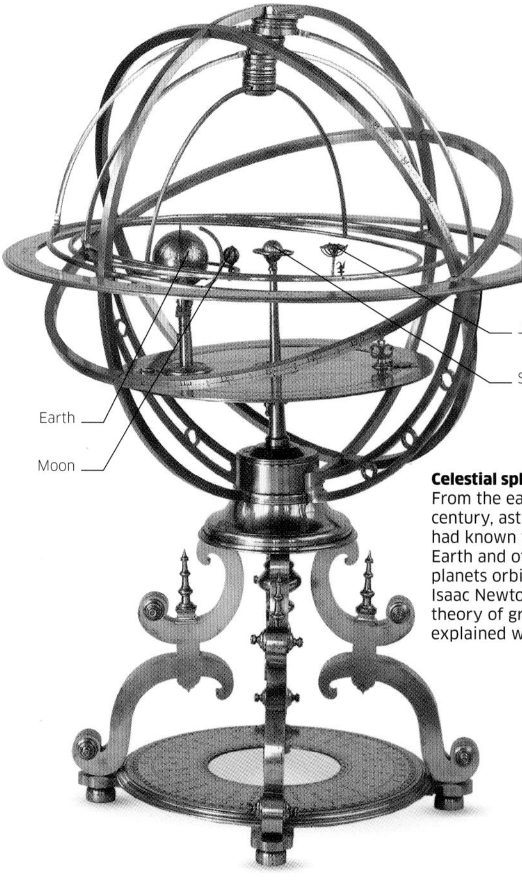

Celestial sphere
From the early 17 century, astronom had known that th Earth and other planets orbit the S Isaac Newton's theory of gravity explained why.

Rights of Man—and Woman

As well as scientific advances, the Enlightenment was marked by new ideas about society. From around 1750, a group of radical philosophers in France began to spread ideas that questioned traditional thinking. They argued that kings, nobles, and clergymen did not deserve special rights and privileges over other people. Other thinkers such as Jean-Jacques Rousseau and Mary Wollstonecraft produced powerful arguments calling for all human beings to be treated equally, while writers such as Voltaire and Montesquieu wrote satires (mocking imitations) of corrupt institutions and outdated opinions.

1748

A French thinker named Charles-Louis de Secondat, known as Montesquieu, published *Spirit of the Laws*, which called for political power to be divided between the monarchy, parliament, and the courts of law—a system known as the "separation of powers."

1759

Candide, a satirical novel by French philosopher Voltaire, highlighted the hardships and injustices suffered by many people around the world. Voltaire wrote that, for people to be truly free, they had to be able to use the power of reason, and they had to know and defend the basic rights of all human beings.

1762

Swiss philosopher Jean-Jacques Rousseau proposed that governments should only rule with the consent of the people. In *The Social Contract*, he wrote, "Man is born free, and everywhere he is in chains."

37 percent—the drop in value of South Sea Company stocks when the venture collapsed in 1720.

9 The number of symphonies written by Romantic composer Ludwig van Beethoven.

19

‹evolution of wealth

,mong the new concepts to develop at this time was the science of conomics, or the study of wealth and money. Great empires grew ich by trading goods across the world. Banks offered a safe place for ne wealthy to deposit their money, and gave loans to people who eeded funds to start new businesses. Ordinary people were also ncouraged to invest in money-making projects. Financial projects ometimes went disastrously wrong: for example, in 1720, when ne British South Sea Company collapsed, taking with it millions of ounds (dollars) of investors' money.

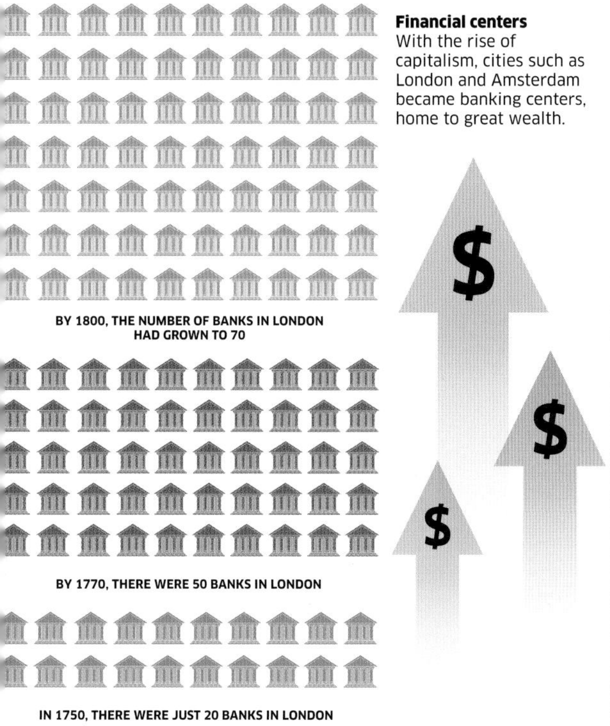

BY 1800, THE NUMBER OF BANKS IN LONDON HAD GROWN TO 70
BY 1770, THERE WERE 50 BANKS IN LONDON
IN 1750, THERE WERE JUST 20 BANKS IN LONDON

Financial centers
With the rise of capitalism, cities such as London and Amsterdam became banking centers, home to great wealth.

LABOR WAS THE FIRST PRICE, **THE ORIGINAL PURCHASE-MONEY** ˉHAT WAS PAID FOR ALL THINGS. **T WAS NOT BY GOLD OR BY SILVER, BUT BY LABOR, THAT ALL THE WEALTH OF THE** VORLD WAS ORIGINALLY PURCHASED."
ADAM SMITH, SCOTTISH ECONOMIST, 1776

1776
English-American Thomas Paine published a pamphlet, *Common Sense*, which supported America's independence from Britain. His later work, *Rights of Man*, argued that people should overthrow the government if it abuses their rights.

1792
Englishwoman Mary Wollstonecraft called for women to receive the same education and opportunities as men in *A Vindication of the Rights of Women*. She imagined a society based on the rule of reason, which respects all human beings.

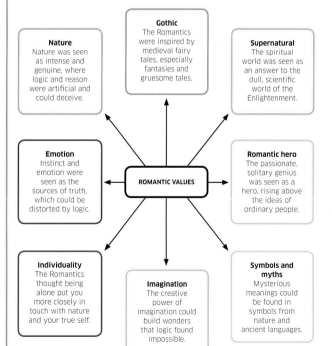

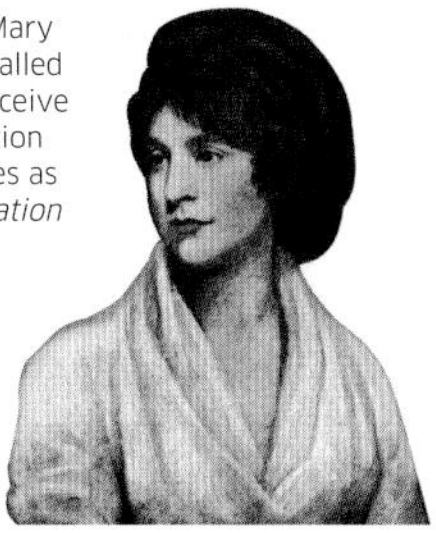

Burning of the Houses of Lords and Commons
Romantic artists such as Englishman Joseph Turner painted images depicting the power of natural forces. This painting shows a fire that swept through the British Houses of Parliament in 1834.

Romantic rebellion

The ideals of the Enlightenment spread quickly, but by the late 18th century they had already inspired a backlash, especially among artists, musicians, and poets. A new movement, Romanticism, arose, arguing that total reliance on reason ignored the values of emotion and natural beauty. Famous Romantics include the composer Beethoven, writers such as John Keats and Edgar Allan Poe, and painters such as Eugène Delacroix.

ROMANTIC VALUES

- **Nature** Nature was seen as intense and genuine, where logic and reason were artificial and could deceive.
- **Gothic** The Romantics were inspired by medieval fairy tales, especially fantasies and gruesome tales.
- **Supernatural** The spiritual world was seen as an answer to the dull, scientific world of the Enlightenment.
- **Emotion** Instinct and emotion were seen as the sources of truth, which could be distorted by logic.
- **Romantic hero** The passionate, solitary genius was seen as a hero, rising above the ideas of ordinary people.
- **Individuality** The Romantics thought being alone put you more closely in touch with nature and your true self.
- **Imagination** The creative power of imagination could build wonders that logic found impossible.
- **Symbols and myths** Mysterious meanings could be found in symbols from nature and ancient languages.

Patriot soldiers had to buy their own weapons and gear.

The American Revolutionary War

In the 18th century, Britain ruled 13 colonies along the east coast of North America. From 1770, these colonies began to rebel against British control and, 13 years later, they won their independence.

Britain's colonies in North America were governed from London. Their inhabitants were British citizens, but were not given full rights: they could not vote and had no one representing their views in parliament. The colonists were angry about this unfair treatment, but the British ignored their concerns, passing unpopular laws and putting high taxes on everyday goods such as sugar, tea, and paper.

In 1775, tensions erupted into war. A large, well-trained British army invaded from Canada in 1777, to support British troops stationed in the colonies, but they were outmaneuvered by skillful American commanders led by George Washington. The war ended with the British defeated, and the creation of a new independent country: the United States of America.

The Continental Army

From 1775, the American forces began to organize their volunteer troops into a regular army. George Washington was determined to train a force to rival the well-trained British soldiers, and formed the Continental Army. For much of the war the men were poorly paid and equipped, but they nevertheless achieved a number of stunning victories.

Disciplined volley

One of the key skills an army needed was the ability to fire the muskets all together a volley. This require training and disciplir so that the soldiers c not fire too early as enemy advanced.

Lead-up to the war

Britain had run up huge debts during the Seven Years War (1756–63), and urgently needed money to pay them off. The government planned to raise the money by taxing its American colonies. The colonists protested against this taxation without representation, and the revolutionary idea of becoming free of British rule spread. In 1773, the British imposed a harsh new tax on tea, and colonists in Boston took action. They boarded a ship in the harbor and threw chests of British tea into the sea. This event, famous as the Boston Tea Party, lit the fuse for the war. The British responded by imposing restrictive new laws on the colonies, and especially on Boston. The Continental Congress—a group of representatives of the 13 colonies—called these laws intolerable acts and sent messages of protest to the king.

AT THE BOSTON TEA PARTY, **COLONISTS DESTROYED 342 CHESTS OF TEA** WITH A VALUE OF **ABOUT $15,000.**

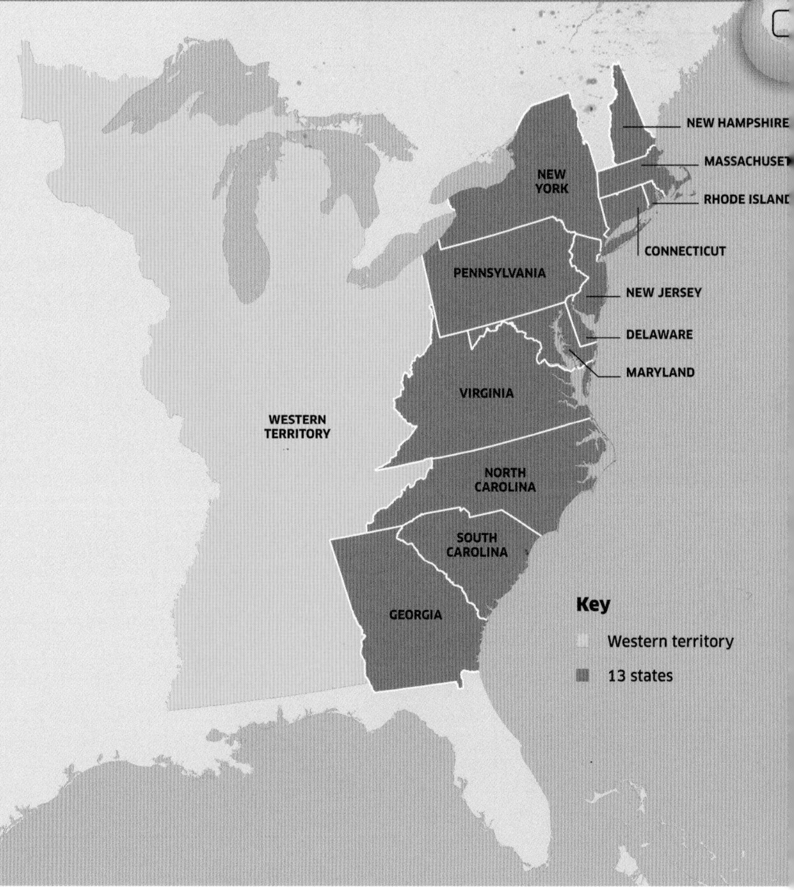

The new nation

At the end of the war, the 13 colonies that had fought for independence became the first states of the US. They signed a peace treaty with Britain in 1783, which also granted them ownership of substantial territory to the west.

2.5 million—the population of the colonies, less than one-third of Britain's.

Boys as young as 10 fought in the American army, and women served as nurses, cooks, and even spies. 21

he Declaration of Independence

he 13 rebel colonies formed their own overnment, the Continental Congress, which oon decided to seek complete independence om Britain. A lawyer from Virginia named homas Jefferson was given the task of rafting a Declaration of Independence to formalize their position. The argument of the Declaration was based on four key points, listed below. On July 4, 1776, representatives of the 13 colonies signed the Declaration to form a new nation: the United States of America.

Right to rebel That colonies must be allowed to sever eir connection with their rulers as long as ey have good reasons and can explain them.

Legitimate government That the only acceptable form of government one that tries to do the best for its people and spects their rights.

Crimes of the king That the British king had ruled the colonies ithout respecting the rights and interests the people who lived there.

Declaration of independence That, therefore, the colonies had a right throw off the government of the British nd rule themselves, and were no longer art of the British Empire.

"WE HOLD THESE TRUTHS **TO BE SELF-EVIDENT,** THAT ALL MEN ARE CREATED **EQUAL, THAT THEY ARE** ENDOWED BY **THEIR CREATOR** WITH CERTAIN **UNALIENABLE RIGHTS,** THAT AMONG THESE ARE **LIFE, LIBERTY AND THE PURSUIT OF HAPPINESS."**

DECLARATION OF INDEPENDENCE

ommander-in-chief

eorge Washington was a tobacco farmer and ained surveyor from Virginia who gained military xperience fighting against the French in North merica during the Seven Years War. His opposition Britain's treatment of its American colonies led his appointment as commander-in-chief of the bel American army. Washington turned his men to a professional fighting force. He held them gether during tough times and lost battles, and d them to victory. In 1789, he was elected as the rst President of the United States of America.

atue of Washington
ashington is often referred to as e father of the nation because of s leadership and influence in the unding of the United States.

he two sides

e American forces relied heavily on militia—cal groups who organized themselves into ghting units. The Continental Army was also pported by French and Spanish troops, and me Native Americans. The "redcoats" of the itish army were assisted by Loyalists (colonists who wanted to remain part of the British Empire), German mercenaries, and Native Americans, who wanted to protect trading and territory agreements with the British. The British navy controlled the coast, but could not affect the war inland.

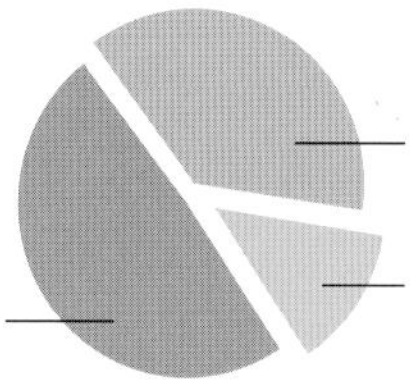

AMERICANS AND ALLIES

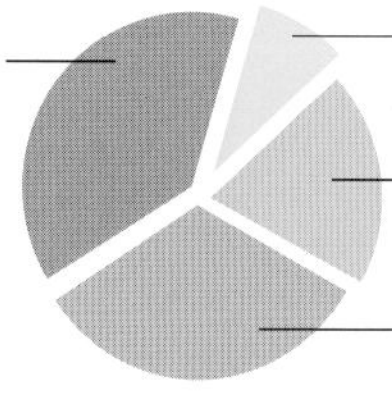

BRITISH AND ALLIES

The march to independence

Nearly all of the early battles of the American Revolutionary War ended in a draw. The British forces were too powerful for the Americans to defeat outright, while the colonial forces used local support and knowledge of the land to escape attacks by the British. As the war went on, however, stronger leadership and assistance from foreign allies tipped the balance in favor of the Americans, and the British suffered crushing defeat.

1773

The road to rebellion
After the colonists destroyed shiploads of British tea in Boston harbor, the British tightened their control on the colonies by passing laws to limit their freedoms. It was the final straw, and two years later, the first shots of the Revolutionary War were fired.

BELT OF A LOYALIST SOLDIER, WITH ROYAL INSIGNIA

April 1775

The first battle
British troops marched to Concord, Massachusetts, to raid the colonists' store of weapons. The colonists sent a force to resist them. Although they were forced to withdraw, the Americans succeeded in blocking the British and protecting their supplies.

Autumn 1777

Battle of Saratoga
More than 6,000 British soldiers were surrounded and forced to surrender by the Continental Army. This resounding American victory encouraged the French to join the war on the American side, followed by the Spanish and the Dutch.

Winter 1777

Valley Forge
With foreign support on the way, the American army sought shelter in a defensive camp at Valley Forge, near Philadelphia. Although safe from British attack, they suffered from harsh conditions and lack of supplies throughout the winter months. An estimated 2,000 men died of disease and starvation.

October 1781

Victory for the colonists
After several further defeats, the British were forced to retreat to the east coast. As the American army and the French navy closed in, the British were trapped at Yorktown, Virginia, and surrendered. The war was over and the Americans had won.

1783

Peace treaty
After long negotiations, a peace treaty was finally agreed in Paris in September 1783. Britain handed over large areas of territory to the US, and also signed separate treaties with the Americans' European allies, France, Spain, and the Netherlands.

PROPOSED MODEL FOR THE FIRST UNITED STATES SILVER DOLLAR, 1777

Rioting men in France sometimes dressed as women, because female rioters were punished less severely.

French Revolution

In 1789, the French monarchy was overthrown in a bloody revolution. The rebels created a government run by the citizens rather than the nobility, but rivalry between its members brought chaos and bloodshed.

At the end of the 18th century, France was nearly bankrupt after a series of costly wars. To make matters worse, a bad harvest in 1788 left much of the population short of food. While the country faced starvation, King Louis XVI and the nobility lived in luxury, and rumors spread that they were hoarding grain that the poor desperately needed. The French people had heard how the Americans overthrew the rule of the British king in 1776, and as the poor grew more dissatisfied, they demanded change. In 1789, a sharp rise in the price of bread caused riots on the streets of Paris, and when the king demanded a rise in taxes that same year, the people took action and the French Revolution began.

An unequal society

French society was split into three classes, called Estates. The First Estate, the clergy, and the Second Estate, the nobility, were extremely wealthy. Although they made up only 3 percent of the population, they owned 40 percent of the land and paid almost no taxes. The remaining 97 percent of the population made up the Third Estate, common people ranging from merchants and craftsmen to poor country farmers. Their taxes paid for the wealthy lifestyle of the rich. All three Estates had representatives in the government assembly, the Estates General. On June 17, 1789, the representatives of the Third Estate decided to set up their own government, the National Assembly.

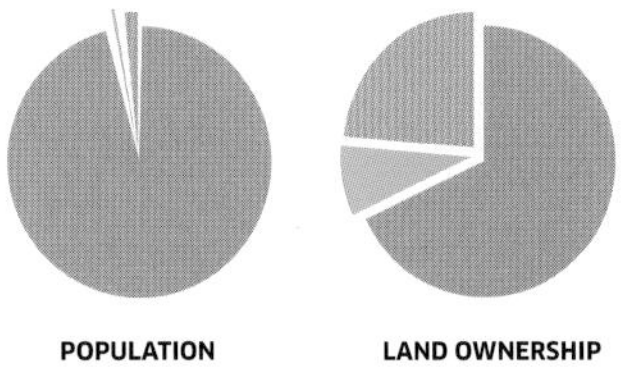

The end of the monarchy

The new National Assembly promised to give power to the people, leaving the king as only a figurehead. When rumors spread that the king had ordered the army to close down the new government, the citizens formed a National Guard to fight back. Their first target was the Bastille, a prison where enemies of the old government were held, which they stormed on July 14, 1789. Many of the king's supporters fled or joined the revolution, and the king himself was imprisoned in the Tuileries Palace in Paris. He tried to regain favor with the people by agreeing to their demands for reform, but remained a hated figure. On August 10, 1792, his palace was stormed by the mob and the king was sent to prison. In 1793, he was found guilty of plotting against the French people and sentenced to death by beheading.

***The Taking of the Tuileries Palace*, 1792**
On August 10, 1792, a mob stormed the Palace of Tuileries, where the king and queen were living, and arrested them, ending the French monarchy. This painting depicts the overwhelming numbers of the revolutionaries, who far outnumbered the Swiss Guards protecting the palace.

The Bastille was nearly empty when it was stormed. Only seven prisoners were rescued, but 98 revolutionaries died in the attack.

Timeline

The French Revolution saw France change from a monarchy, ruled by the king, to a Republic, in which power was held by the people, although suspicion and brutality left many living in fear. The end of the Revolution saw the rise of a new emperor.

June 14, 1789
The King of France, Louis XVI, asked the government to approve an increase in taxes. Already angered by a national food shortage and unfair taxes, representatives of the Third Estate (the working people) broke away from the other two Estates. They announced their intention to govern the country themselves, and formed a National Assembly.

July 14, 1789
Rumors spread that the king had called for the army to shut down the new National Assembly. Angry mobs began to riot throughout Paris, bringing chaos to the city. A crowd stormed the Bastille prison, liberating seven inmates. This date came to be known as the beginning of the Revolution, and July 14 is celebrated as a national holiday in France to this day.

October 5, 1789
A crowd of about 7,000 women marched on the royal palace at Versailles, outside Paris, to protest over the shortage of bread. According to later rumor, when she heard the people lacked bread, the French queen, Marie Antoinette, said "Let them eat cake." This was taken as a symbol of how little the monarchy understood the sufferings of the people.

10 The number of **days in a week** in the new **revolutionary French calendar.**

1.6 million—the **number of soldiers** in **Napoleon's army** at its height.

23

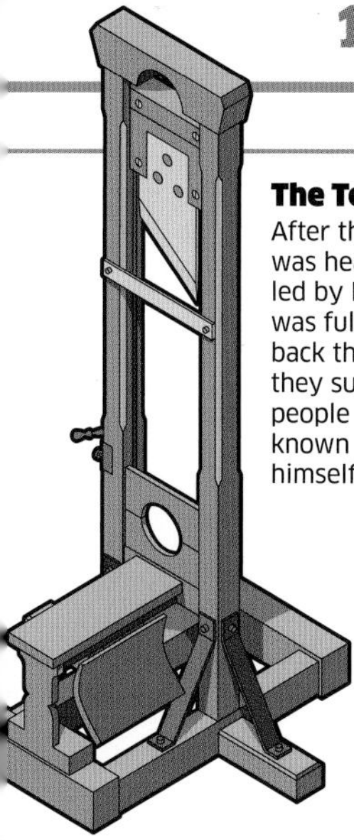

The Terror

After the death of the king in 1793, the National Assembly was headed by a group called the Jacobins, a political club led by Maximilien de Robespierre. They believed that France was full of spies sent by foreign powers who wanted to bring back the monarchy. The Jacobins began to execute anyone they suspected of working against them. Around 40,000 people were killed in Paris alone during this bloody period, known as The Terror, which only ended when Robespierre himself was sent to the guillotine in 1794.

The guillotine
This gruesome machine was used during the French Revolution to execute people as quickly and efficiently as possible.

THE GUILLOTINE WAS NICKNAMED THE **"NATIONAL RAZOR"** **AND WAS USED TO EXECUTE** UP TO 20 PEOPLE A DAY.

he ideals of the Revolution

ne new Republic of France was influenced by the United States, which had on independence from Britain in 1776. Like the Americans, the French evolutionaries wrote out a document, the "Declaration of the Rights of Man nd the Citizen," which would underpin the new government. It proclaimed at all men and women are born equal, so kings and nobles have no right to le over those of common birth, and that people should be allowed to overn themselves by democratic vote. These ideas remain important to eories of democracy and human rights to this day.

aximilien de Robespierre
ench lawyer Maximilien e Robespierre was at the refront of the Revolution. e believed passionately equal rights and vernment by the people. owever, he betrayed his vn beliefs by deciding the ly way for the Revolution succeed was by the aths of those who posed it. Tens of ousands of so-called nemies of the Revolution" ere executed on the ders of Robespierre d his allies.

The Napoleonic Wars

After the Revolution, France was left without a strong leader and surrounded by enemies. In 1800, Napoleon Bonaparte (1769–1821), a young general, became a hero to the people after a series of stunning military victories. In 1804, he made himself Emperor of France, and began a campaign of conquest across Europe. From 1805–1807, his armies defeated Austria, Russia, and Prussia until his empire covered most of Europe. He was finally defeated in 1815 at the Battle of Waterloo by an alliance of the nations of Europe.

UNIFORM

MUSKET

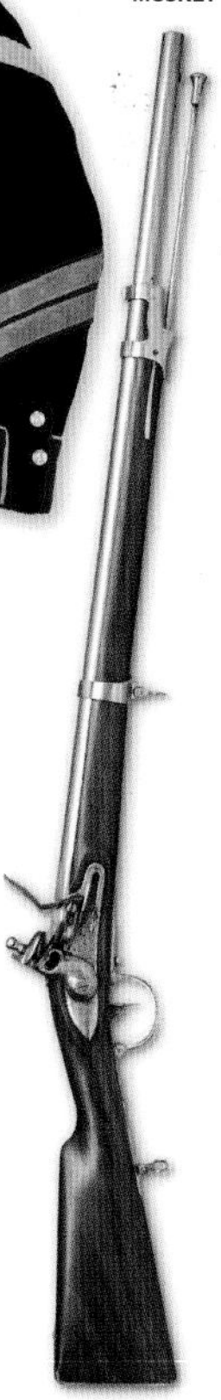

French infantryman's uniform
Napoleon's soldiers were the most feared in Europe. They were superbly trained and operated in tight formations. Their uniform consisted of white breeches, dark blue jacket, and a hat, or shako, decorated with a red plume. Each man was armed with a large, heavy gun called a musket.

e 25, 1791
king and queen attempted to flee the ntry in disguise. They were spotted taken back to Paris, where they were under guard in the Tuileries Palace. y were moved to prison in 1792 and, 793, they were executed by guillotine r being accused of helping Austria, queen's homeland, which was at war Revolutionary France.

1792–1801
France's neighbors were outraged by the overthrow and death of King Louis. They also hoped to gain control of French lands in the confusion of the Revolution. Wars broke out between France and other European countries such as Austria, Italy, and Britain, and in French overseas territories such as Haiti. The French armies emerged victorious.

Spring 1793
A Committee of Public Safety was founded by Maximilien de Robespierre to fight back against agents of the old government, thought to be secretly undermining the Revolution. The Committee ran out of control, accusing many innocent people of betraying the Republic. As many as 40,000 people were executed during this Reign of Terror.

December 2, 1804
Napoleon Bonaparte proclaimed himself Emperor of France and was crowned in Paris. A military genius, he had become enormously popular among the French people after winning a stunning series of victories during the wars of 1792–1801. After his coronation, Napoleon's armies begin a war of conquest across Europe, winning great success at first.

7 The average age at which children were sent to work in the 1800s.

The Industrial Revolution

Between 1760 and 1860, an age-old way of life based on farming and crafting by hand was transformed, as people moved to towns and goods were produced by machines in factories.

This transformation began in Britain, where ingenious inventors and engineers applied new scientific ideas to the old methods of farming, mining, and manufacturing. Britain also had a ready supply of raw materials, such as coal and iron ore, to power the new inventions, and a rapidly growing population eager to work in the factories and buy the new goods they produced. The Industrial Revolution transformed our way of life, bringing incredible wealth to some, but crushing poverty to many others.

Faster travel

Industrial factories depended on being able to bring in large quantities of raw materials (such as coal and cotton fiber) and send out large quantities of finished products. The old methods of transportation—such as wagon trains and sailing ships—could not move materials quickly enough or in large enough amounts. Industrial countries built huge networks of canals, where barges carrying up to 33 tons were pulled along by horses. Rail networks and steam engines allowed people and goods to travel quickly over long distances. Steam ships made ocean journeys far quicker and more reliable.

Steam locomotives

The railway became one of the greatest symbols of the Industrial Revolution. From around 1840, the US led the world in producing fast, reliable steam locomotives, such a this one built in 1863 by the Baltimore and Ohio Railroad.

New machines

The backbone of the Industrial Revolution came from new machines. Cotton making, for example, had been a lengthy process involving hours of hard work. Inventions such as the Spinning Jenny (1764), and the Spinning Mule (1779) could do the work automatically in a fraction of the time. At first, these bulky machines were powered by water wheels, and so were built-in factories next to rivers. The first water-powered cotton mill was built by entrepreneur Richard Arkwright in 1771 in Derbyshire, England. Over time, water wheels were replaced by steam engines, and factories moved into towns.

Water-powered cotton mill

Cotton is made by combing out fluffy fibers and spinning them into thread. Before the Industrial Revolution, this was done by workers in their own homes. Cotton mills could process much larger amounts of cotton far more quickly.

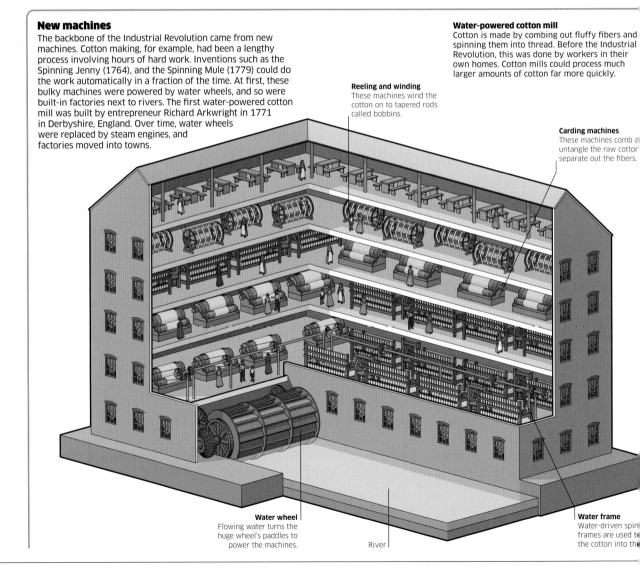

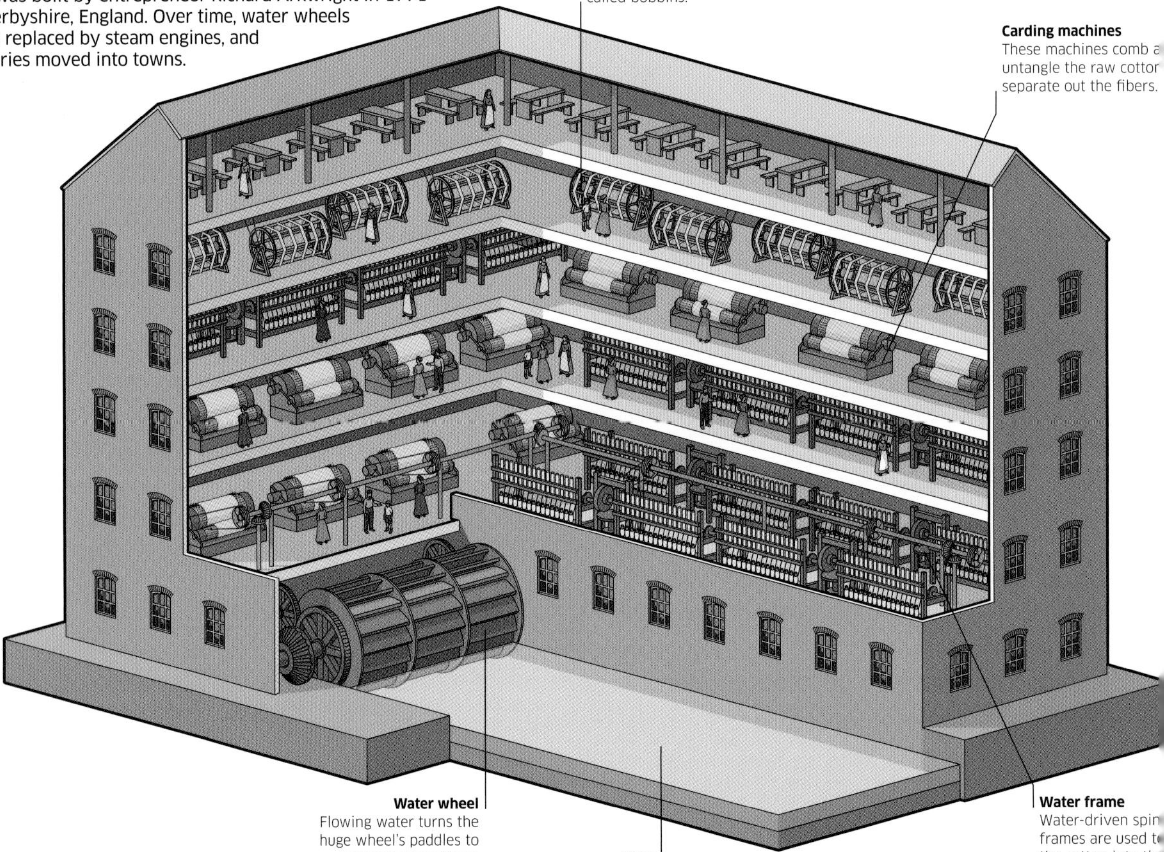

Reeling and winding
These machines wind the cotton on to tapered rods called bobbins.

Carding machines
These machines comb a untangle the raw cottor separate out the fibers.

Water wheel
Flowing water turns the huge wheel's paddles to power the machines.

River

Water frame
Water-driven spin frames are used t the cotton into th

5 million tons—the amount of coal mined in 1850 in Britain.

The new spinning machines produced cotton 1,000 times more quickly than a human worker.

4,000 miles (6,400 km)—the length of new canal built in Britain from 1760–1840.

25

NO. 117 THATCHER PERKINS LOCOMOTIVE

ᵒoverty in towns

ndustrial progress brought great wealth to actory owners and entrepreneurs, and made asic goods such as food and clothing cheaper han ever before. However, it also created a ew kind of poverty. Large numbers of people noved to the cities in search of work, where hey were packed into crowded, dirty housing. Many were unemployed and ended up in rison for debt, or forced to move into harsh odgings called workhouses, where they erformed hard labor for no pay. Those who id have jobs worked in unsafe conditions. hey were often paid poorly, and many amilies struggled to afford basic essentials.

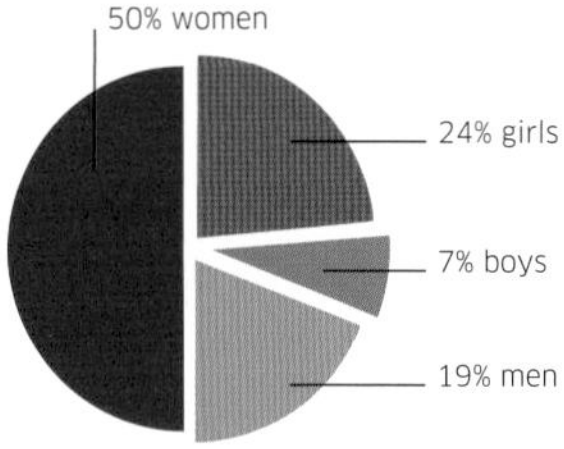

Workers in a cotton mill, 1859
A third of workers in the mills were children, aged as young as five. Some worked for 12 hours a day, and dangerous accidents were common.

ʀise of the machines

he changes brought by industry quickly athered momentum across Europe and orth America. New factories created heap goods and jobs for poor laborers. t the same time, mechanized farming eft many rural workers unemployed, and orced them to move to cities to work in factories. With so many people looking for work, factory owners offered low wages, which meant laborers looked for even cheaper goods. Scientists and entrepreneurs used their profits to built new machines and factories, bringing prices down and creating more jobs.

Science
New discoveries give scientists ideas about better ways to do things. They develop new technologies such as steam power and cheap steel.

→ **Invention**
Engineers and inventors experiment with new scientific ideas, using them to develop machines that make farming and manufacturing easier.

→ **Mechanization**
Business owners invest money in the new inventions. Farms and workshops use machines instead of human workers, and factories are built.

↓ **Migration to cities**
Machines replace many jobs on farms. At the same time, new factories create jobs in cities. Laborers move from the country into cities to find work.

← **Lower wages**
In crowded cities, many people compete for jobs. Business owners pay low wages, since it is hard for their employees to find work elsewhere.

← **Demand for low prices**
Poor workers need food and goods to be cheap. This encourages business owners to build more factories and find cheaper ways of working.

↑ (back to Science)

An island of ideas

The many inventions of the 18th century were made possible by scientists and engineers, funded by rich entrepreneurs. Together they developed new machines, such as the steam engine, new ways of working, such as factory mass production, and new industrial processes, such as the Bessemer process for producing steel.

1701–1831

Farming with machines

A growing population called for more food and more efficient ways to grow it. In 1701, English inventor Jethro Tull created a seed drill that automatically sowed crops. Steam-powered plows appeared in the 1820s, and the American engineer Cyrus McCormick designed a mechanical harvester in 1831.

SEED DRILL

1771

The first factories

Richard Arkwright built the first water-powered mill in Derbyshire, England. Fast-flowing water created enough power to run his spinning machines. This allowed cotton to be mass-produced, since more thread could be made much faster. Arkwright became a pioneer of modern factories.

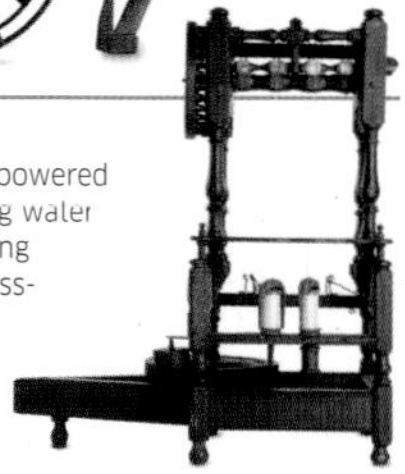

ARKWRIGHT SPINNING FRAME

1776

Watt's steam engine

Inventors across the world had experimented with using steam to power machinery for hundreds of years, with little success. In 1776, Scottish inventor James Watt built a much more efficient engine, which could provide an up-down movement for pumping and a circular movement for operating machines.

WATT'S ENGINE

1779

Bridges of iron

The era of modern bridge-building started in 1779 with the construction of the Ironbridge in Shropshire, England, the first bridge to be made entirely of solid cast iron. With stronger bridges and better-quality iron and steel, bridges could be built over longer distances, opening up new routes for roads and railways.

1790

Gas lighting

Gas from coal mines was burned in lamps to provide lighting in streets and homes. It was pumped through a network of pipes across major cities. The large-scale introduction of gas lighting in the 1790s was the work of William Murdoch, a Scottish engineer who also built steam engines. Gas lighting was brighter and more reliable than candles and oil lamps, allowing factories to remain open all night.

GAS STREET LIGHT

1833

Brunel and the railways

Isambard Kingdom Brunel was a bridge and railway engineer who oversaw the creation of much of Britain's rail network. At age 27 he became engineer to the Great Western Railway, where he constructed over 1,000 miles (1,600 km) of track. He was famous for his innovative designs for bridges, viaducts, and tunnels.

1855

The steel revolution

In 1855, an Englishman named Henry Bessemer discovered a new, cheap way of making steel, using a machine called a "Bessemer converter" to burn impurities out of iron. Steel was essential for building railways, machinery, factories, and vehicles. By making it cheap and widely available, Bessemer's new process opened the way for a huge increase in the rate of industrialization.

The course of the war

The war pitted 23 Union states of the North and West against 11 Confederate states of the South. The North had superior numbers, wealth, and weaponry, and despite some brilliant military successes, the South was eventually forced to surrender.

1. **April 12, 1861**
   Tensions between the North and South were running high. The war began when the Confederate army shot at Union soldiers stationed at Fort Sumter, South Carolina, and forced them to lower the American flag in surrender.

2. **July 21, 1861**
   The Confederates won their first battle near a small stream in Virginia called Bull Run. The Union answered by blockading the ports and borders of southern states, trying to wreck their economy.

3. **September 16–18, 1862**
   The Battle of Antietam, one of the bloodiest of the war, left 23,000 soldiers dead, wounded, or missing. The Confederates were beaten back in a turning point of the war.

4. **May 18–July 4, 1863**
   The city of Vicksburg beside the Mississippi River, held by the Confederates, was taken by Union troops. Control of the Mississippi was vital, since the South was using it to transport food and soldiers.

5. **July 1–3, 1863**
   In Gettysburg, Pennsylvania, the Union won the largest battle of the war after three days of fighting. Confederate leader General Lee lost 20,000 men, who were killed or wounded.

6. **April 9, 1865**
   With his troops surrounded, General Lee surrendered to General Ulysses S. Grant in a house in the village of Appomattox, Virginia.

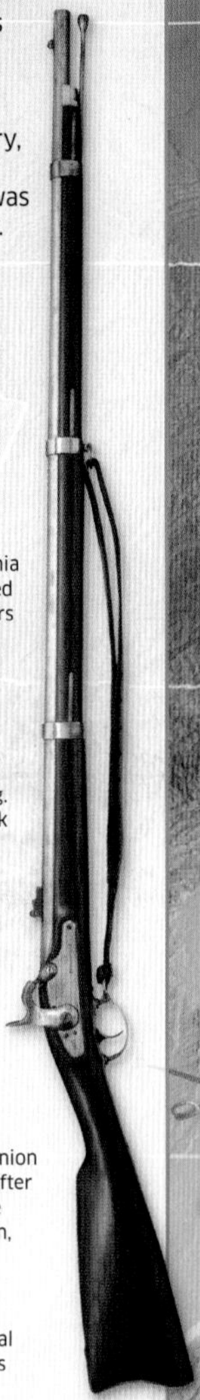

SPRINGFIELD RIFLE MUSKET 1861

Abraham Lincoln

The 16th president of the United States, Abraham Lincoln was a brilliant orator. He was determined to keep the states of America together at all costs. After the war, he hoped to heal the divide between North and South, but was killed by a supporter of the South while at the theater in 1865.

> **"GOVERNMENT OF THE PEOPLE,** BY THE PEOPLE, **FOR THE PEOPLE** SHALL NOT PERISH FROM THE EARTH."
>
> ABRAHAM LINCOLN, SPEECH TO UNION FORCES AT GETTYSBURG, 1863

The Confederacy

Eleven Southern states broke away from the Union to form the Confederacy: North Carolina, South Carolina, Georgia, Alabama, Mississippi, Louisiana, Florida, Texas, Tennessee, Arkansas, and Virginia. They fought for states' rights and the right to own slaves. The Confederates had their own capital in Richmond, Virginia, and their own currency, flag (see left), and president–Jefferson Davis.

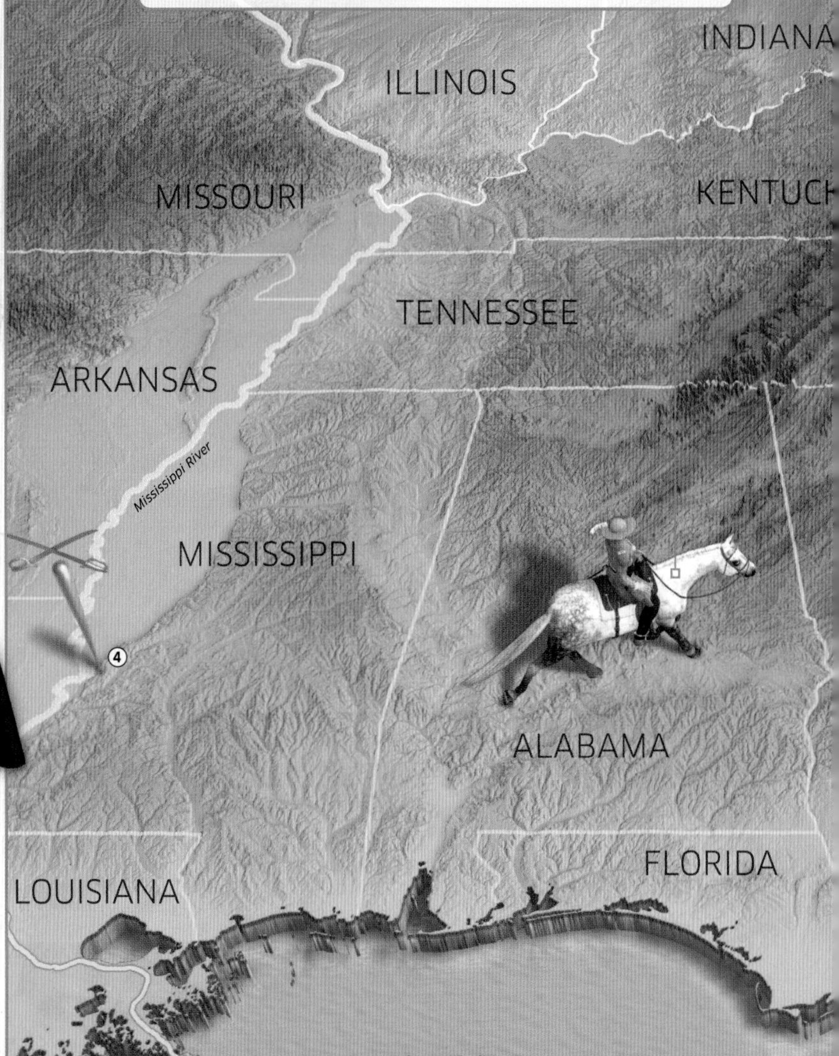

A nation divided

Battles were fought across America, but most of the fighting occurred in the states of Virginia and Tennessee, and along the border states–slave states that did not declare independence. Much of the conflict was near the Confederacy's capital, Richmond, Virginia, and the Union capital in Washington, DC.

2 The number of **Union** soldiers for every one **Confederate** soldier.

The number of **Americans killed** in the **Civil War** is nearly **equal** to the number who died in every other **foreign war** fought by the US since.

27

Union blockade
The Union set up a naval blockade in the Atlantic and Gulf of Mexico to stop trade to Southern ports.

Artillery
Both sides in the war used artillery fire to cause huge numbers of casualties among enemy troops.

The Union
The Union of the northern states, led by President Abraham Lincoln, had a larger army, including 200,000 freed slaves who joined the fight. They also had greater resources. Victory over the South meant more than the ending of slavery: the United States stayed together as one nation with one government. However, the process of rebuilding the war-torn country would be long and hard.

The Civil War

The election of Abraham Lincoln as president in 1860 tore the US in half, and the Civil War broke out between the North and South over the rights of individual states and the issue of slavery.

The US had been one country made up of many states, but in the mid-19th century it became a divided nation. The northern states, made strong by industry and immigrants from Europe, had little sympathy for the old-fashioned farm culture of the South, which depended on slavery. The people of the South suspected that the North was seeking to destroy their way of life. When Abraham Lincoln became president, 11 Southern states feared he would abolish slavery and left the Union. The war that followed divided families and friends. More than 620,000 soldiers died, and even though the country was finally reunited, bitterness remained for decades.

World War I

Half a century of power struggles, in which Germany and Austria-Hungary were set against France and Russia, ended with four years of bloody conflict that involved nearly every country in the world.

The war that followed was fought mainly in Europe, but fighting also spread to the Middle East, Africa, and Asia. Nations took part in bombing raids and chemical warfare, as well as experimenting with tanks, military aircraft, and submarines. However, most of the war was fought using ordinary artillery, machine guns, rifles, and horses. What was different about this war was the vast numbers of those involved: soldiers fought and died in the millions, and entire populations were expected to help make weapons and support the war.

The fronts

The areas, or fronts, in which the war was fought went right across Europe. The two main zones, or theaters, of war were the Western Front and the Eastern Front. The Western Front stretched from the North Sea to the Swiss border and was made up of a continuous line of trenches. The Eastern Front, on the other side of Europe, saw the great armies of Germany and Austria-Hungary battle against Russia.

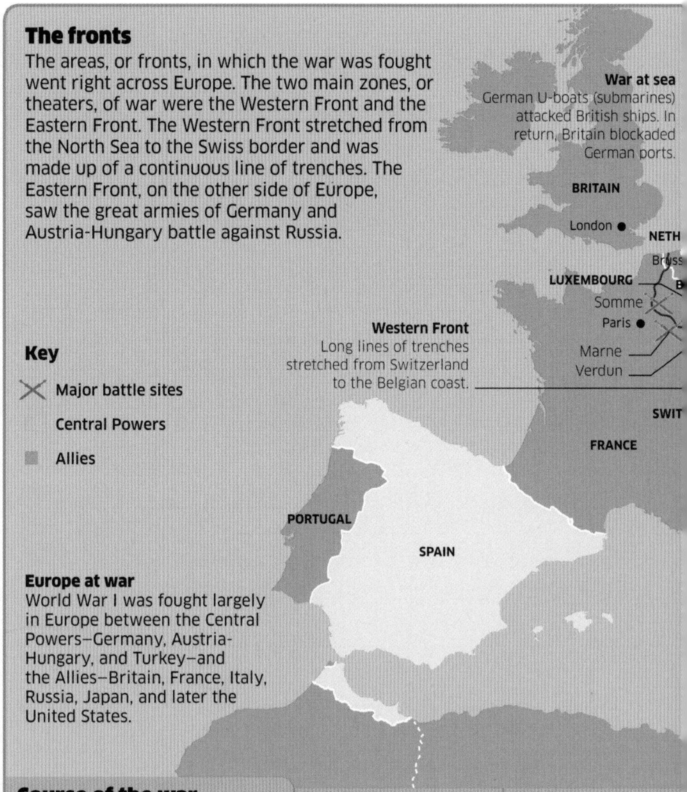

War at sea
German U-boats (submarines) attacked British ships. In return, Britain blockaded German ports.

Major battle sites

Europe at war
World War I was fought largely in Europe between the Central Powers–Germany, Austria-Hungary, and Turkey–and the Allies–Britain, France, Italy, Russia, Japan, and later the United States.

Causes of the war

On June 28, 1914, the Archduke of Austria-Hungary was shot by a nationalist from Serbia in the Balkans. Austria-Hungary blamed Serbia for the killing and declared war. Russia offered to support Serbia. Germany declared war on Russia, then on France. Country after country rushed to defend their allies or declare war on their rivals until armies were on the move across the world. Most people believed the war would be over very quickly, but they were tragically mistaken.

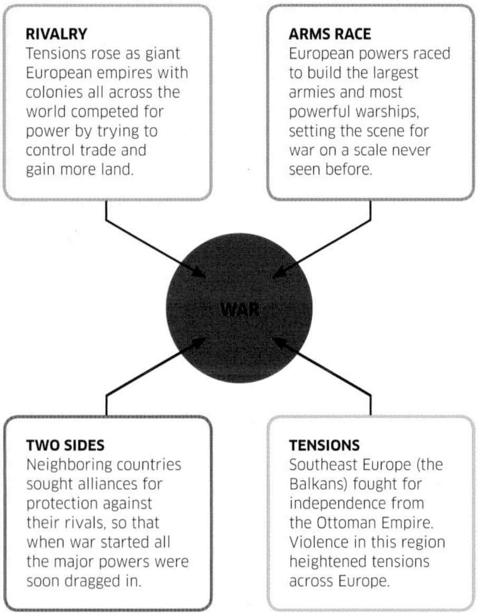

RIVALRY
Tensions rose as giant European empires with colonies all across the world competed for power by trying to control trade and gain more land.
ARMS RACE
European powers raced to build the largest armies and most powerful warships, setting the scene for war on a scale never seen before.
WAR
TWO SIDES
Neighboring countries sought alliances for protection against their rivals, so that when war started all the major powers were soon dragged in.
TENSIONS
Southeast Europe (the Balkans) fought for independence from the Ottoman Empire. Violence in this region heightened tensions across Europe.

Road to war
In the early 1900s, powerful European nations competed for trade and land, and built up large armies. Nations made agreements to support one another (alliances), but these were often fragile. Two groups of countries on opposite sides emerged: the Central Powers and the Triple Entente (Allies).

Course of the war

For four long years bloody battles were fought. The Western Front, running across eastern France, saw some of the heaviest fighting. Until 1917, Germany and the Central Powers seemed to be winning, but that changed when the US came to fight for the Allies.

1914
Tannenberg
The Germans won an early great victory against Russia at the Battle of Tannenberg in August 1914, capturing 125,000 men. Meanwhile, Germany invaded neutral Belgium to attack France, which they hoped to defeat quickly. British forces arrived to support Belgium and France.

1914
LUXEMBOURG
Marne
Long lines of trenches stretched from Switzerland to the Belgian coast.
Germany's invasion of France was halted at the River Marne, just east of the French capital city, Paris. This left Germany and Austria-Hungary faci attacks from both east ar west. Both sides suffered huge losses in open battl and began to build trenc systems for defense.

The war at home

World War I was the first "total" war, meaning not just soldiers but the whole civilian population were involved. The entire nation was expected to help keep the war effort going, by helping on the "Home Front." Civilians only received fixed rations of food to make sure enough could be sent out to the troops, and women took over many of the jobs of men sent to fight. Bombing raids on German, French, and some British cities brought the war into ordinary homes.

ВСЕ ДЛЯ ВОЙНЫ!
ВОЕННЫЙ ЗАЕ

RUSSIAN POSTE

Everyone must play their part
This Russian poster reads: "All for the war." In wartime, women took men's places on farms, in factories, and in offices. Every man was expected to fight: military leader Lord Kitchener (far right) calls on British men to join the army.

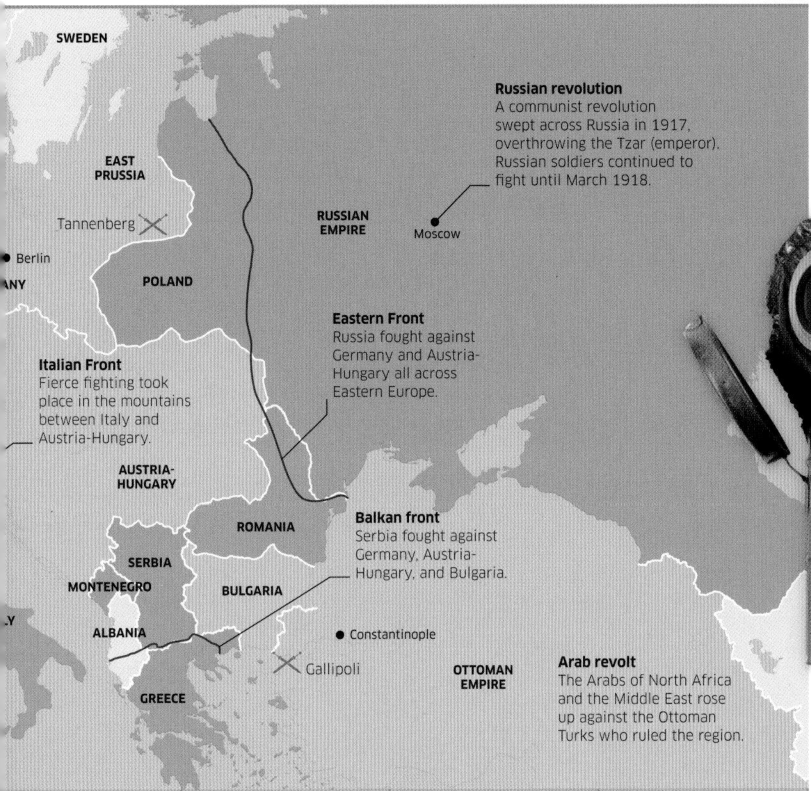
SWEDEN
EAST PRUSSIA
Tannenberg
Berlin
ANY
POLAND
RUSSIAN EMPIRE
Moscow
Russian revolution
A communist revolution swept across Russia in 1917, overthrowing the Tzar (emperor). Russian soldiers continued to fight until March 1918.
Eastern Front
Russia fought against Germany and Austria-Hungary all across Eastern Europe.
Italian Front
Fierce fighting took place in the mountains between Italy and Austria-Hungary.
AUSTRIA-HUNGARY
ROMANIA
Balkan front
Serbia fought against Germany, Austria-Hungary, and Bulgaria.
SERBIA
MONTENEGRO
BULGARIA
.Y
ALBANIA
Constantinople
Gallipoli
GREECE
OTTOMAN EMPIRE
Arab revolt
The Arabs of North Africa and the Middle East rose up against the Ottoman Turks who ruled the region.

15–16

llipoli
tish Empire forces, luding many troops m Australia and New aland, launched an ack on the Ottoman pire at Gallipoli, on west coast of Turkey. ey landed in April 1915, suffered heavy ualties and were ced to withdraw.

1916

Verdun
Continuous fighting across the trenches produced a stalemate on the Western Front. Trying to break the deadlock, Germany launched an attack on the French fortifications at Verdun. After months of brutal fighting, the exhausted French army forced the Germans to retreat.

1916

Somme
The British and French, after little progress for two years, began the Big Push —a large-scale attack to break through German lines at the Somme in France. Thousands were mown down by German machine guns. More than 600,000 Allied troops were killed or wounded, for little gain.

1918

Hundred Days Offensive
Provoked by German submarine attacks on American ships, the US entered the war in 1917. In 1918, American, British, and French soldiers mounted a series of successful attacks, known as the Hundred Days Offensive, forcing the Central Powers to surrender.

A new kind of warfare

At the start of the war, armies on both sides were still using outdated tactics, such as cavalry and bayonet charges. However, with deadly weapons like machine guns widely available, these old tactics failed, resulting in huge numbers of deaths. By the end of the war, both sides had developed new strategies, as well as new weaponry, such as aircraft. Both sides used poison gas to kill off enemy soldiers. Horses, shown to be unsuited to the modern battlefield, were replaced by the first tanks.

GERMAN GAS MASK AND CONTAINER

Mustard gas symbol

GERMAN GAS SHELL

Poison gas
At first there was no protection against poison gas, but by the middle of the war both sides carried gas masks. Around 30 types of gas were used, causing more than 1.2 million casualties.

230 **The number of soldiers that perished each hour throughout the four-and-a-quarter years of the war.**

'YOU
ARE THE MAN
I WANT'

SH POSTER

The cost of the war

There had never before been a human conflict on this scale, and with it came huge cost to human life. More than half of the 65 million men who fought across the world were killed or wounded, and many died of disease. More than six million ordinary citizens died, from illness or starvation. Europe was left in ruins, and its systems of government, and the way people worked and lived, changed forever.

Military deaths
It is estimated that 15 million people died in World War I. Most of them were soldiers, especially in the armies of Russia and Germany.

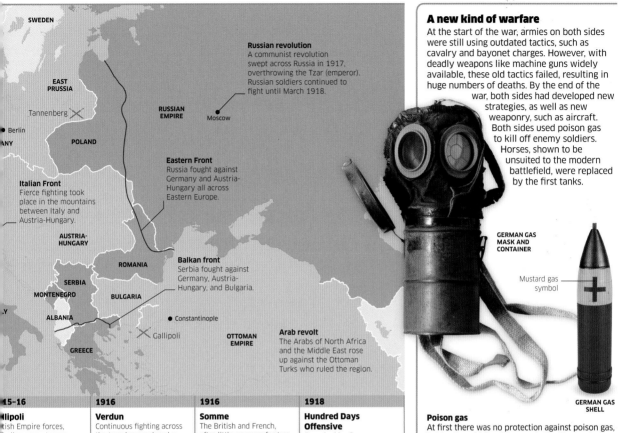

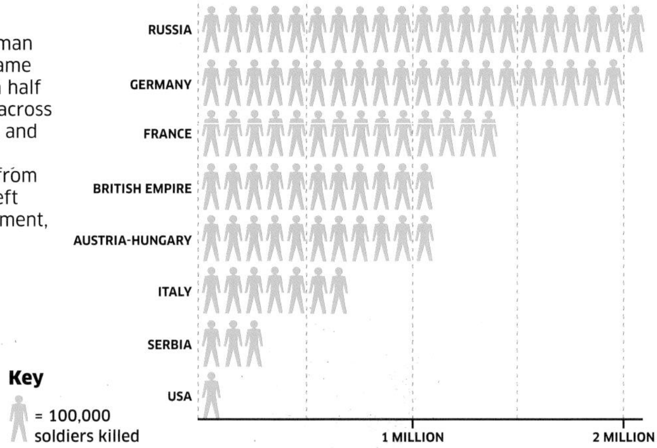
RUSSIA
GERMANY
FRANCE
BRITISH EMPIRE
AUSTRIA-HUNGARY
ITALY
SERBIA
USA
1 MILLION
2 MILLION
Key
= 100,000 soldiers killed

1.5 million children died during the Holocaust.

57 The number of consecutive nights London was bombed during the Bli

World War II

In September 1939, Germany, led by brutal dictator Adolf Hitler, stormed into Poland. This was the beginning of World War II. Lasting six long years, it was the deadliest conflict in history.

World War I was supposed to be "the war to end all wars," but defeated countries believed they had been treated badly by harsh peace terms. In the 1930s, a catastrophic global recession broke out, which left many people poor and destitute. Disillusioned, they began to turn to new, forceful leaders for solutions.

In Germany, the Nazi Party rose to power under Adolf Hitler. He launched mass invasions west into Europe and east into the USSR in search of more "living space" for the German people. At the same time, the Japanese fought to take control of Asia and the Pacific Ocean. The battle to defeat Germany, Japan, and their allies would spread across the globe, and cost the lives of millions.

Nazi symbol
This German army badge shows an eagl on top of a swastika- the symbol of the National Socialist German Workers Party (Nazis), led by Adolf Hitler.

Rise of Fascism

Fascism, a new form of nationalism, rose out of the ashes of World War I. As people struggled with mass unemployment and poverty, they were drawn to strong leaders such as Benito Mussolini (Italy) and Francisco Franco (Spain) who promised national unity and prosperity. In Germany, Adolf Hitler declared himself Führer (leader) and led the country to war.

Codes, spies, and propaganda

World War II was one of the first wars fought with modern technology and electronics. Both sides became very good at spying, and they used codes to pass on secret information. Spies and double agents did their best to outwit the enemy. In their own countries, they used posters, movies, and radio broadcasts to spread propaganda—powerful messages designed to stir national pride, loyalty, and hatred of the enemy.

Enigma
The Enigma machine was a German device used to send coded messages. It could only be read by another Enigma machine. The British cracked the codes in 1941 using an early form of computer.

Rotator cylinder
Letters are coded by a set of rotating wheels. They can only be decoded using the same settings.

Keyboard
When a letter is pressed, it sends an electrical signal to the rotator for coding.

Plugboard
The plugboard hugely increases the number of coding combinations.

Theaters of war

Battles raged on land, sea, and in the air across Western Europe, the Eastern Front, the Mediterranean, North Africa, and the Pacific and Atlantic oceans. Few nations remained neutral, supporting either the Allies (Britain, France, the US, and Russia) or the Axis (Germany, Italy, and Japan).

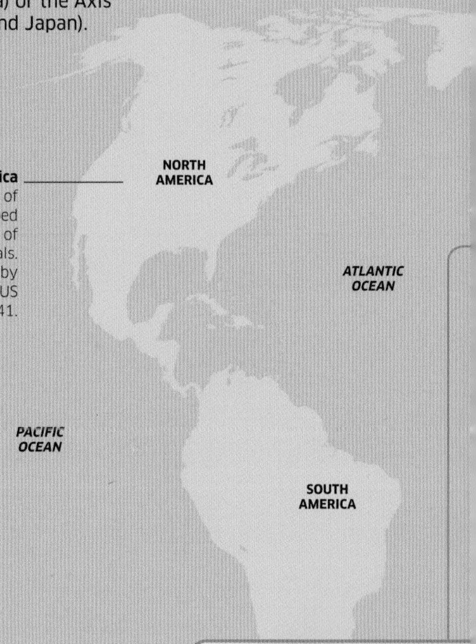

Battle of the Atlan
The Allies needed to keep shippi lanes open, so essential suppli from the US could reach Brita and the USSR. German U-boa (submarines) sank many convoy but the Allies eventually defeat the German nav

United States of America
Neutral at the start of the war, the US helped the Allies with loans of money and materials. A surprise attack by Japan brought the US into the war in 1941.

North Africa
The Axis and the Allies fought in North Africa from 1940 to 1943. British General Bernard Montgomery defeated German Field Marshal Erwin Rommel in tank battles across the desert.

6 million American soldiers served in World War II.
27 million Soviet soldiers and civilians died on the Eastern Front.
35,000 Allied prisoners of war escaped German and Italian prisons during World War II.
31

The Holocaust

Adolf Hitler was convinced that the German people were the "master race" and that other people, such as Jews, were inferior. Under German occupation, Jews were herded into ghettos where many starved to death. In 1942, Hitler instigated the Final Solution–the murder of all Jews. He set up concentration camps where "inferior" people such as Jews, homosexuals, gypsies, and Soviet prisoners of war were gassed to death in one of the most horrific campaigns in human history.

The yellow star
Jews were forced to wear this yellow badge to identify them as Jewish. It became a symbol of Nazi persecution.

"I STILL BELIEVE, IN SPITE OF EVERYTHING, THAT PEOPLE ARE TRULY GOOD AT HEART."
ANNE FRANK, JEWISH VICTIM OF THE HOLOCAUST

Europe
At the start of the war, most of mainland Europe fell to the Germans, whose *Blitzkrieg* (lightning war) tactics proved hugely successful. From 1942–43, the Allies began to fight back.

ASIA
PE
AFRICA
PACIFIC OCEAN
INDIAN OCEAN
AUSTRALIA

The USSR
In 1941, the war widened when Hitler invaded the USSR. Early German successes were overturned by tenacious military and civilian resistance in one of the bloodiest campaigns of the war.

The Pacific
The Pacific theater of war included Japan, China, and Korea, and many small islands in Southeast Asia. The Japanese won early victories, but their advance was halted by the US Navy at the Battle of Midway in 1942.

The course of the war

Hitler's forces quickly conquered large areas of Europe. He then attacked his former allies, the USSR, but was halted by fierce resistance. When the US joined the Allies in 1941, the tide began to turn. German forces were pushed back, and the Japanese were defeated in brutal fighting across Asia and the Pacific.

Sept 1, 1939
German invasion of Europe
Hitler's lightning invasion swiftly conquered Poland. The following year, German troops took Denmark, Norway, Belgium, the Netherlands, and most of France. The British were forced to evacuate 340,000 Allied troops at Dunkirk, France, in May 1940.

1940
Battle of Britain
During the Battle of Britain, German and British aircraft fought for control of the skies. Germany's defeat prevented a land invasion of Britain, but bombers began deadly air raids on British cities.

GAS MASK ISSUED TO CHILDREN IN BRITISH CITIES

June 1941
Operation Barbarossa
The Germans turned on their former allies, the USSR, reaching Moscow and Leningrad. But they were driven back by Soviet counterattacks and the harsh winter. Both sides suffered huge losses, and the Germans suffered their first defeat of the war.

Dec 7, 1941
Pearl Harbor
Japan, Germany's allies, mounted a surprise attack on American ships at Pearl Harbor, Hawaii, bringing the USA into the war. In June 1942, the US fleet defeated the Japanese Navy at the Battle of Midway in the Pacific Ocean, halting the Japanese advance.

Oct 1942
El Alamein
The Allies won a major victory when the British drove the Germans out of Egypt at the Battle of El Alamein.

DESERT RAT BANNER OF BRITISH FORCES IN NORTH AFRICA

Winter 1942
Stalingrad
The focus of the war on the Eastern Front, the brutal Battle of Stalingrad, USSR, involved unimaginable hardship as two armies fought for control of the city. The Soviet Red Army destroyed superior German forces, and soon began to march on Germany.

June 6, 1944
D-Day
After two years of planning, the Allies invaded Europe in Operation Overlord. To liberate France, 4,000 landing craft, 600 warships, and thousands of Allied aircraft hit five beaches in Normandy. Germany was forced to surrender just 11 months later.

Aug 6, 1945
Hiroshima
In the last act of the war, the Americans used a new weapon, the atomic bomb, to force the Japanese to surrender. They dropped bombs on the cities of Hiroshima and Nagasaki. The two explosions killed more than 300,000 people.

18 of the 22 **major cities in North Korea** were **flattened by air raids** in the Korean War.

A world divided

The Cold War saw two superpowers face off, backed by global alliances. The communist nations (marked in red), led by the USSR, were opposed by NATO (marked in blue), an alliance led by the US, and other allied countries around the world.

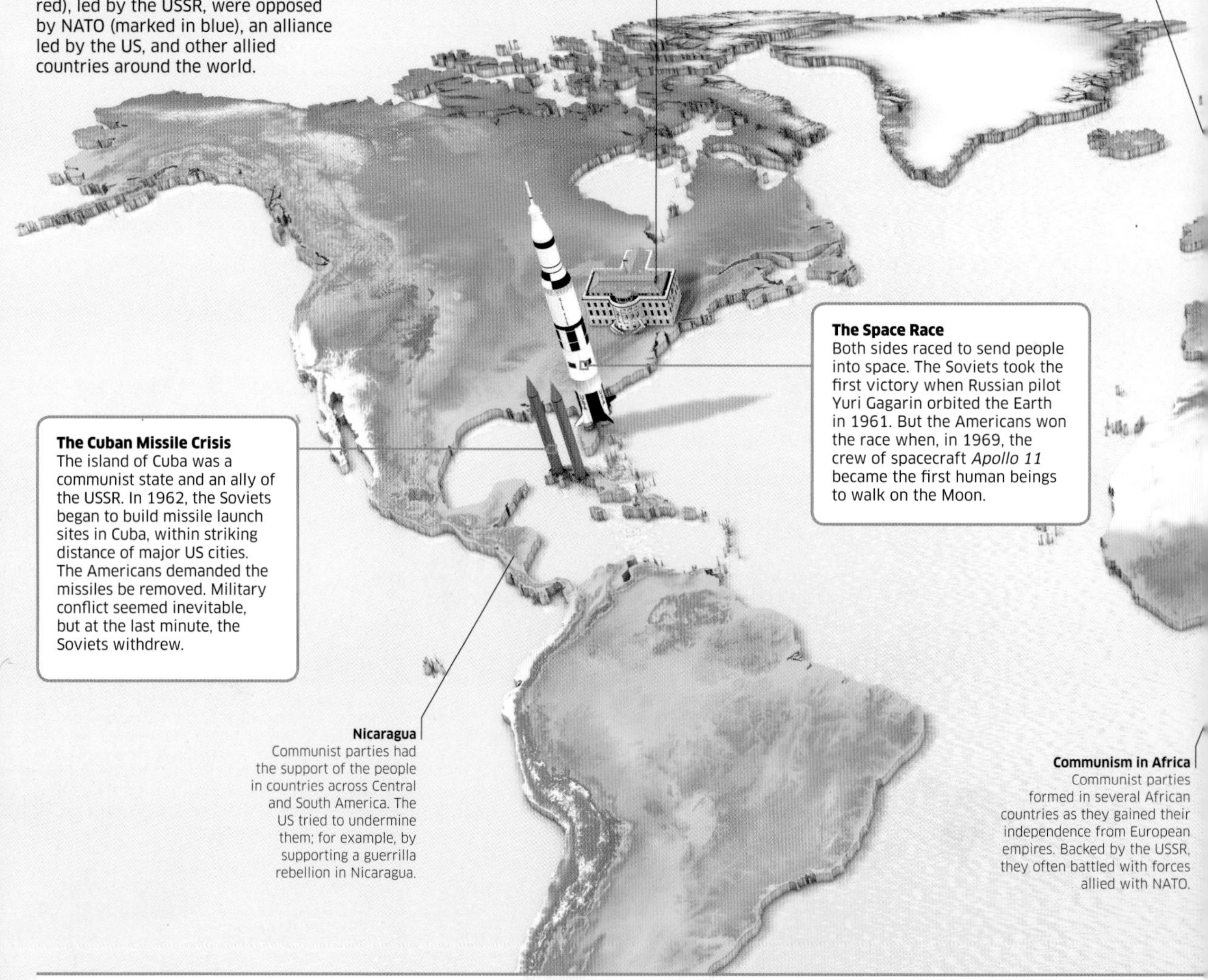

United States of America
The US was the most powerful NATO country. Its leaders worked to destabilize communist states across the world, but were not always successful.

United Kingdom
Allied with the US, the UK had an extensive spy network and its own arsenal of nuclear weapons.

The Space Race
Both sides raced to send people into space. The Soviets took the first victory when Russian pilot Yuri Gagarin orbited the Earth in 1961. But the Americans won the race when, in 1969, the crew of spacecraft *Apollo 11* became the first human beings to walk on the Moon.

The Cuban Missile Crisis
The island of Cuba was a communist state and an ally of the USSR. In 1962, the Soviets began to build missile launch sites in Cuba, within striking distance of major US cities. The Americans demanded the missiles be removed. Military conflict seemed inevitable, but at the last minute, the Soviets withdrew.

Nicaragua
Communist parties had the support of the people in countries across Central and South America. The US tried to undermine them; for example, by supporting a guerrilla rebellion in Nicaragua.

Communism in Africa
Communist parties formed in several African countries as they gained their independence from European empires. Backed by the USSR, they often battled with forces allied with NATO.

Global conflict

The battle between NATO and the USSR spread across the world. An "Iron Curtain" divided Europe between communist east and democratic west. Violent struggles broke out in Africa, Latin America, and Asia. In the end it was economic more than military force that brought the war to an end.

"FROM EACH ACCORDING TO **HIS ABILITY,** TO EACH ACCORDING TO **HIS NEEDS."**
COMMUNIST MOTTO

1945
As World War II came to an end, the Allied leaders arranged to divide Europe between them. The USSR forced Eastern European countries such as Poland and Hungary to turn to communism. By 1948, Europe was divided, with democracy in the west and communist rule in the east.

1948
The German capital, Berlin, in Soviet-controlled East Germany, was partly controlled by the US, Britain, and France. The Soviets tried to squeeze the Allies out by blocking roads and railways. The Americans and British got around the blockade by airlifting in more than a million tons of supplies.

1950
The US government feared that Soviet spies had found their way into key institutions such as the army and intelligence services. A Senator named Joe McCarthy began a campaign to hunt down enemy agents. His search became a witch hunt where innocent people were persecuted.

1956
Hungary, a Soviet ally in Eastern Europe, elected a new leader, Imre Nagy, who promised to reform the communist government. The USSR, determined to keep control of the country, sent tanks to restore Soviet control and remove Nagy from power. Many civilians were injured or killed.

1979
Soviet allies in Afghanistan were attacked by Islamic resistance fighters. The US supplied weapons and training to the rebels, while the USSR sent in an army to back up the communists. The war lasted for almost a decade, and millions of Afghan civilians were forced to flee their homes.

1987
The USSR was faced with economic collap A new leader, Mikhail Gorbach announced a po of openness, reforming the communist government and seeking peace w NATO. In 1989, Gorbachev and US President George HW Bush announced the e of the Cold War.

6 million—the estimated **number of Afghan civilians** forced to **flee their homes** in the **Soviet-Afghan War**, 1979–89.

10 million **Polish people** joined the **Solidarity protest movement** in 1980, undermining communist rule.

The Iron Curtain
At the end of World War II, the USSR took control of much of Eastern Europe, by force where necessary. The dividing line between the two sides became known as the Iron Curtain.

USSR
The revolution of 1917 saw the Russian Empire become the USSR, the world's first communist state.

The Vietnam War
In 1954, Vietnam split into communist North and US-allied South. As tensions rose, the US sent troops to support South Vietnam. They were drawn into a brutal guerrilla war, and were forced to withdraw in 1973. South Vietnam was conquered by the North in 1975.

China
A brutal civil war saw China become a communist nation in 1949. Millions died in the decades of turbulence that followed.

Korea
Communist North Korea, aided by China and the USSR, battled the US and its allies for control of US-allied South Korea from 1950–53.

Sputnik
The USSR took a lead in the Space Race by launching the first man-made satellite, *Sputnik 1*, in 1957.

The Berlin Wall
Germany and its capital, Berlin, were split between the USSR, and the US, France, and Britain. The Soviets built a wall across Berlin to keep people from fleeing to the West. The wall was demolished in 1989 as the Cold War ended.

The Cold War

After World War II, the world was divided between two immensely powerful rivals: the communist USSR and the democratic US. Bitter enemies, these two superpowers faced off, backed by massive arsenals of nuclear weapons.

great reformer
ıail Gorbachev reformed the USSR sought peace with NATO. But he ousted from power in 1991 and USSR split apart.

The people of the USSR (the Soviets) believed in communism, a system that shares all wealth equally. However, their government was often corrupt and oppressive. The US was a capitalist democracy, and its people enjoyed much greater freedom than those in communist countries. Both sides had vast stores of nuclear weaponry, enough to wipe each other out if they ever went to war. This threat of "mutually assured destruction" forced them to fight by other means, using spies and economic warfare to weaken the other's position. Most of their battles were fought in smaller countries such as Vietnam and Nicaragua, with the USSR trying to spread communism and the US fighting to prevent them from succeeding.

5 billion mobile phones were in use globally by 2011.

6.1 billion—population of the wor at the start of the 21st centur

The 21st century

At the end of the 20th century, the world got ready to party. Huge celebrations took place across the globe to greet the year 2000, the start of the new millennium. The new century brought grave new challenges, but also amazing opportunities.

With the world's population expanding, humanity's demands on the planet are growing rapidly. As the 21st century goes on, scientists have become increasingly concerned that we may run out of some natural resources, and that human activity is causing dangerous changes to our environment. Many countries have also had to contend with devastating natural disasters. Terrorist attacks brought fear and conflict to many cities, and a global financial collapse increased the hardship for millions.

At the same time, the 21st century has seen astonishing new advances in technology. Smartphones and tablets have transformed the way we communicate, and the Internet has expanded hugely to give voices to users across the globe.

Digital revolution

The digital revolution began in the 1980s, when computers became cheap enough for people to buy and use at home. At first computers were big metal boxes, but today they are hidden in everyday objects, such as smartphones, tablets, MP3 players, and cameras. The Internet is rapidly evolving to play a central role in society, transforming cultural, economic, and political landscapes. There are thought to be more than 2 billion Internet users worldwide, all of whom can exchange information in an instant.

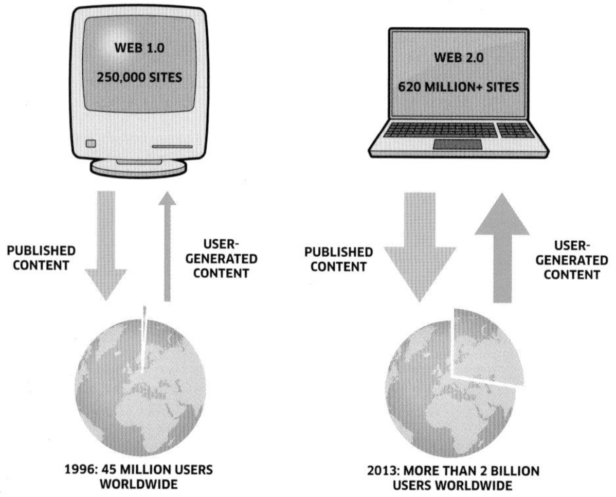

Web use
During the 1990s, most people only used the Internet to look up information. In the 21st century, the amount of user-generated content has hugely increased, with blogs and social networking sites allowing people to share their ideas and experiences.

IN 2001, GOOGLE INDEXED **250 MILLION IMAGES.** IN 2010, IT INDEXED **MORE THAN 10 BILLION.**

The War on Terror

In 2001, a group of Islamist terrorists named al-Qaeda launched a series of attacks on targets in the US. A decade of conflict followed. The US and its allies launched a "War on Terror," invading Afghanistan to capture the terrorists and prevent further attacks. Meanwhile, al-Qaeda and their allies plotted to cause more deaths and destruction in other countries across the world.

Sept 2001

9/11
On September 11, 2001, the suffered devastating terroris attacks. Members of al-Qaed a global terrorist network of radical Muslims, hijacked fou aircraft. They flew two into t World Trade Center in New Y (pictured) and one into the Pentagon. The fourth crashed Pennsylvania. Almost 3,000 people were killed in the atta which shocked the world.

The War in Iraq

In 1991, Saddam Hussein, leader of Iraq, ordered an invasion of neighboring Kuwait. His armies were driven out by an international force led by the US, but tensions remained high. In 2001, the international community suspected that Saddam Hussein possessed weapons of mass destruction capable of causing huge civilian casualties. As the War on Terror heightened tensions across the Middle East, the US and UK led an invasion of Iraq in 2003, toppling Saddam Hussein from power. Although the invasion lasted only a few weeks, violence would continue in Iraq for many years.

Saddam Hussein's statue is toppled
US tanks rolled into the Iraqi capital, Baghdad, in April 2003, signaling the end of the dictatorship of Saddam Hussein. Jubilant Iraqis toppled a massive statue of the former leader in a symbolic gesture of contempt.

Natural disasters

The first years of the 21st century were beset by natural disasters and extreme weather. In 2003, more than 40,000 people died in heat waves across Europe. In 2004, a huge tsunami caused devastation around the Indian Ocean, killing almost 230,000 people in 14 countries. The following year, a powerful storm, Hurricane Katrina, laid waste to the city of New Orleans, with wind speeds of 125 mph (200 kph). A massive earthquake devastated the island of Haiti in the Caribbean in 2010, killing more than 300,000 people and leaving millions homeless. In 2011, another earthquake triggered a tsunami in Japan, destroying homes and causing radioactive material to leak from the Fukushima nuclear power plant.

Global dangers
Countries all across the world experienced devastating natural disasters in the early years of the 21st century. Some were freak chance events, while others have been linked to changes in the world's climate.

Oct 2001

Invasion of Afghanistan
The US and its NATO allies launched Operation Enduring Freedom after the 9/11 attacks, in an effort to track down Osama bin Laden. The terrorist leader was thought to be in Afghanistan, where the Taliban government was allied with al-Qaeda. The invasion succeeded in overthrowing the Taliban, but violence continued in Afghanistan for years.

March 2004

Madrid bombings
On the eve of Spanish political elections, members of al-Qaeda exploded bombs on four trains in Madrid, killing 191 people and wounding 1,841. The Spanish government had supported the 2003 US-led invasion of Iraq. The Spanish public promptly voted that political party out of office and installed a party that withdrew Spanish troops from Iraq.

July 2005

London bombings
Britain experienced attacks on July 7, 2005, when terrorists carried out a series of suicide bombings on London's transport system. Three bombs exploded on underground trains, and one on a double-decker bus. An al-Qaeda website claimed that they had launched these attacks in retaliation for Britain's involvement in the wars in Iraq and Afghanistan.

May 2011

Death of Bin Laden
US President Barack Obama received intelligence that Osama bin Laden, the head of al-Qaeda, was hiding out in a compound in Abbottabad, Pakistan. In a daring night raid named Operation Neptune Spear, a US Navy Seal team shot dead bin Laden and four others. It was an important milestone in the War on Terror, but not an end to Islamist extremist terrorist attacks.

The Arab Spring
In 2010, a Tunisian man set fire to himself in protest to poor treatment by the Tunisian police. His rebellion sparked a wave of unrest that spread across the Arab world, in countries ruled by dictators or corrupt and oppressive governments. First, the Tunisian leader, Zine al-Abidine Ben Ali, was forced from power. Then dissent spread to Egypt, where President Hosni Mubarak resigned after massive popular protests. In 2011, there were uprisings in Yemen, Bahrain, Libya, and Syria. Libya's leader, Colonel Muammar Gaddafi, was overthrown by rebel fighters. Free elections took place in some Arab countries, but others such as Syria were thrown into civil war.

Wave of protest
Demonstrations in Tunisia spread to countries across the Middle East and North Africa.

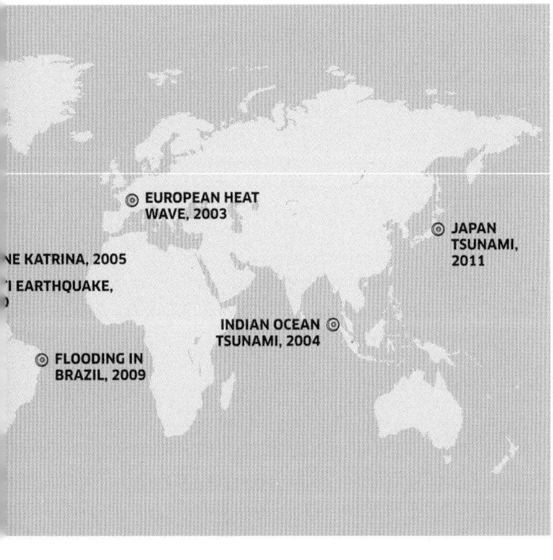

Global financial crisis
In 2007, US banks realized that they had lent money for home mortgages to hundreds of thousands of customers who could not afford to pay them back. To make matters worse, the banks had bundled up the mortgages with other investments, worth billions of dollars. These suddenly lost value, threatening financial systems across the world. The value of investments plummeted, and huge banks collapsed in the US and Europe. The crisis brought poverty and unemployment to many countries across the globe.

2009 financial statistics
- Value of world's companies wiped out
- GDP (annual production) of US
- Money spent by European governments to prop up banks in debt

Losses and bailouts
The crisis wiped 33 percent off the value of the world's companies. Governments were forced to pay out huge sums of money to keep their economies afloat.

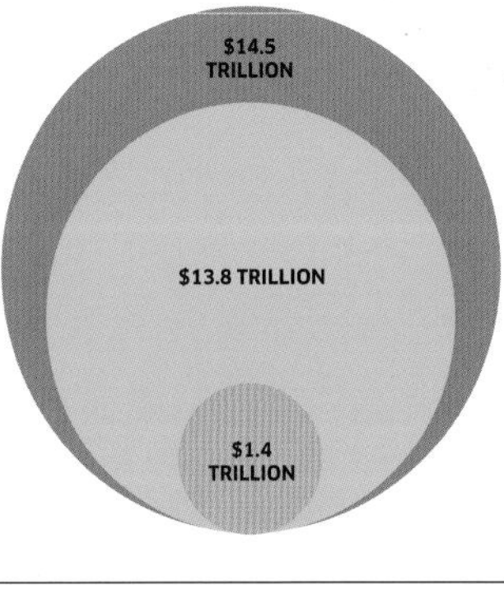

Index

Page numbers in **bold** type refer to main entries

A

Afghanistan 35
Age of Enlightenment 18–19
al-Qaeda 34, 35
antibiotics 15
Antietam, Battle of 26
apartheid 15
Apollo spacecraft 32
Arab Spring 35
architecture 2, **9**, 13
armor (military) 12
Asia
  empires 14
  Ottoman Empire 3, 29
  Silk Road 2
Atlantic, Battle of 30
Aztecs 3, **6–7**

B

Baghdad 34
banking systems 19, 35
Barbarossa, military operation 31
bin Laden, Osama 35
Blitzkreig 31
bombs 31, 35
Boston Tea Party 20, 21
Britain, Battle of 31
British Empire 14, 20
Bull Run, Battle of 26

C

canals 24
capstans 4
caravels 4
Caribbean 5
Catholicism 2
celestial sphere **18**
cell phones 34
chainmail 12
Christianity
  Church 2
civil rights 15
Civil War **26–27**
civil wars 11, 33, 35
classes (society) 22
colonies (political) 3, 14, **20–21**, 28
Columbus, Christopher 2, **4–5**
communism 14, **32–33**
compasses 5
computers 34
Confederacy, United States 26, 27
Constantinople 3
Continental Army 20, 21
Continental Congress 20, 21
cotton mills 24
Crimean War 14
Cuban Missile Crisis 32

D

da Vinci, Leonardo 2
D-Day 31
death 6
decks, ship 4
Declaration of Independence 21
democracies 23, 32–33
digital technology 34
diseases 15
Drake, Sir Francis 2

E

earthquakes 34
Eastern Front 28
economies 35
Egypt
  Arab Spring 35
El Alamein, Battle of 31
Elizabeth I, Queen of England 2
emperors
  Chinese 11
  Mughal 12, 13
empires
  Asian empires 3
  European empires 14, 28
  Ottoman empire 2
engineering 25
Enigma machine 30
Enlightenment **18–19**
environmental changes 15
equality 15, 18–19, 23
Erasmus, Desiderius 2, 9
estates (class system) 22
estrogen 177
Europe 35, *see also* France; Germany; Spain
executions 23

F

factories 24, 25
Fahrenheit scale 233
farming 25
Fascism 30
France 2, 14, 15, 18
  wars in 28, 29, 30
French Revolution 14, **22–23**

G

Gagarin, Yuri 32
Gallipoli, Battle of 28
Gama, Vasco de 2
Gandhi 14
garrisons 10
gas lights 25
Germany 15, 28–29, **30–31**, 33
Gettysburg, Battle of 26
Gorbachev, Mikhail 32, 33
Grant, General Ulysses S. 26
Great Wall of China 10–11
guillotines 23
gunpowder 12
guns 23

H I

Habsbergs, royal family 2
Han dynasty 11
Hinduism 12, 13
Hiroshima 31
Hitler, Adolf **15**, 30, 31
Holocaust 31
hourglasses 5
human sacrifice 6
Hundred Days Offensive 28
Hussein, Saddam 34–35
Incas 3, **6–7**
India **12–13**
Industrial Revolution 15, **24–25**
internet 34
Iraq war 34–35
Iron Curtain 32, 33
Islamism 34
Italy 8, 9

J L

Jacobins 23
Japan 3, 14, 30, 31
Jews 31
Judaism 31
Latin America 14
latitudes 5
Lepanto, Battle of 3

M

McCarthy, Joe 32
McCormick, Cyrus 25
Machiavelli, Niccolò 9
machines 24
Madrid terrorist attack 35
Magellan, Ferdinand 2
Marne, Battle of 28
Marx, Karl 14
Mayans 6, 7
Medici, royal family 9
Mexico 14
militia 21
Ming dynasty 3, 11
Mississippi River 26
Mohács, Battle of 3
Mughal empire 3, 12
Mussolini, Benito 30

N O

Nagasaki 31
Napoleon Bonaparte, Emperor 23
Napoleonic Wars 14, **23**
NATO 32
natural disasters 34
nature, in art 19
navigation systems **5**
Nazis 30, 31
Newton, Isaac **2**, **18**
9/11 terrorist attacks 34–35
Opium Wars 14
Ozone Layer 15

P

Pacific, theater of war 31
Pearl Harbor attack 31
perspective (art) 8
Peru 6
philosophers 18
poison gas 29
poverty **25**, 30, 35
printing presses **9**, 18
propaganda 30
Protestantism 2

Q R

Qing empire **3**, 11
railways 24, 25
Reformation 2
religions 8
republics 22
revolutions (political) 14, 20–21, 22–24
Rome, ancient
  influence of 8, 9
Russia 14
  USSR 15, **32–33**

S

sacrifice, human 6
Samurais 3
Saratoga, Battles of 21
sculptures 9
sea routes 2
Serbia 28
7/7 terrorist attacks 35
Seven Years War 14, 20, 21
signals
  towers 10
Silk Road 2
slave trade **16–17**, 26, 27
social networks 34
Somme, Battle of 28
Song dynasty 11
South Africa 15
South America 14
space exploration
  Space Race 32
Spain 2, **4**
  empire **3**
  Inca invasion 6, 7
  Madrid terrorist attacks 35
spies 30
Sputnik satellite 33
Stalingrad, Battle of 31
steel 25
supernatural 19
swastikas 30

T

Taj Mahal 12, 13
Taliban 35
Tang dynasty 11
Tannenberg, Battle of
taxation 20, 22
tea 20
telephones 34
telescopes 2
Tennessee 26
terra-cotta warriors 1
terrorism 34–35
theaters (war) 28, **30–**
Triangular Trade 16
tsunamis 34
Tunisia 35
21st Century 34–35

U V

unemployment 30, 35
uniform, military 23 *s*
  also armor (militar
Union, United States 2
  27
United Kingdom 32
United States of Ameri
  15, 16, 34
USSR 14, 15, 31, **32–3**
  also Russia
vanishing points 8
Verdun, Battle of 28
Vicksburg, Battle of 2
Vienna, Siege of 3
Vietnam War 33

W

wars 15, 23
  American 20–21, 26
  China 11
  Iraq 34–35
  Napoleonic 23
Washington, George 20, 21
weapons 29
  bombs 31, 35
  cannon 27
  guns 23
  of mass destruction
  nuclear 33 *see also* Cuban Missile Crisi
Western Front 28
women's rights 15, 19
workhouses 25

Acknowledgments

Smithsonian Project Coordinator: Kealy Wilson.
Smithsonian Enterprises: Kealy Wilson, Product Development Manager; Ellen Nanney, Licensing Manager; Brigid Ferraro, Director of Licensing; Carol LeBlanc, Senior Vice President.
Reviewers for the Smithsonian: *National Museum of Natural History:* Dr. Don E. Wilson, Curator Emeritus, Department of Vertebrate Zoology; Sally Kuhn Sennert, USGS/Global Volcanism Program, Department of Mineral Sciences; Dr. Jeffrey E. Post, Geologist and Curator-in-Charge, National Gem and Mineral Collection; Dr. Nancy Knowlton, Sant Chair of Marine Sciences; Dr. Michael Brett-Surman, Museum Specialist for Fossil Dinosaurs, Reptiles, Amphibians and Fish, Department of Paleobiology; Thomas F. Jorstad, Paleobiology Information Officer, Department of Paleobiology; Dr. Gary Krupnick, Head of the Plant Conservation Unit, Department of Botany; Dr. Christopher L. Mah, Research Collaborator, Department of Invertebrate Zoology; Gary F. Hevel, Research Collaborator, Department of Entomology; Jeremy F. Jacobs, Collections Manager, Division of Amphibians and Reptiles; Christopher M. Milensky, Museum Specialist, Division of Birds, Department of Vertebrate Zoology; Dr. M. G. (Jerry) Harasewych, Research Zoologist and Curator of Marine Mollusks, Department of Invertebrate Zoology; Jim Harle, Map curator volunteer; Dr. Briana Pobiner, Paleoanthropologist and Educator, Human Origins Program; Salima Ikram, Egyptology Unit Head, Department of Anthropology; Dr. William W. Fitzhugh, Curator of Archaeology and Director of Arctic Studies Center, Department of Anthropology; J. Daniel Rogers, Curator of Archaeology, Department of Anthropology; *National Portrait Gallery:* James G. Barber, Historian; *National Air and Space Museum:* Dr. F. Robert van der Linden, Chairman, Aeronautics Division; Roger Connor, Curator, Aeronautics Division; Andrew Johnston, Geographer, Center for Earth and Planetary Studies; *National Museum of African American History and Culture* Ester Washington, Director of Education; *Freer Gallery of Art and Arthur M. Sackler Gallery;* Dr. Alexander Nagel, Assistant Curator of Ancient Near East; James T. Ulak, Senior Curator of Japanese Art; J. Keith Wilson, Curator of Ancient Chinese Art; Debra Diamond, Associate Curator of South and Southeast Asian Art; *National Museum of American History, Kenneth E. Behring Center* David K. Allison, Associate Director for Curatorial Affairs; Dwight Blocker Bowers, Curator, Division of Culture and the Arts; Roger E. Sherman, Associate Curator, Division of Medicine and Science; Ann M. Seeger, Deputy Chair and Curator, Division of Medicine and Science; Dr. Paul F. Johnston, Curator, Division of Work and Industry; L. Susan Tolbert, Deputy Chair and Curator, Division of Work and Industry; Jennifer Locke Jones, Chair and Curator, Division of Armed Forces History.

The publisher would like to thank the following for their kind permission to reproduce photographs:

(Key: a-above; b-below/bottom; c-center; f-far; l-left; r-right; t-top)

2 Dorling Kindersley: The Science Museum, London (bl). **3 Bridgeman Images**: British Library, London, UK © British Library Board (clb); **5 Dorling Kindersley**: The Science Museum, London (fbr); James Stevenson / National Maritime Museum, London (br). **National Maritime Museum, Greenwich, London**: (crb). **8 Corbis**: The Gallery Collection (b). **9 Dorling Kindersley**: Robbie Polley (cl). **Getty Images**: Karl Weatherly / Photodisc (bl). **11 Dorling Kindersley**: The Trustees of the British Museum (crb); David Gower / The Trustees of the British Museum (cr); Alan Hills / The Trustees of the British Museum (fcra, tr, br). **12 Dorling Kindersley**: Board of Trustees of the Royal Armouries (fcra, tr, cr). **14 Getty Images**: OFF / AFP (bl). **16 Dorling Kindersley**: Ray Moller / Wilberforth Collection, Hull Museums (cl). **17 Dorling Kindersley**: Royal Geographical Society, London (bl); Wilberforce House Museum, Hull (cra). **18 Alamy Images**: The Art Archive (clb). **Corbis**: Stefano Bianchetti (br); Lebrecht Music & Arts (bc). **Dorling Kindersley**: National Maritime Museum, London (cr). **19 Corbis**: Lebrecht Music & Arts (bc); Michael Nicholson (fbl);
Philadelphia Museum of Art (tr). **20 Getty Ima**
Brendan Smialowski (cra). **21 Dorling Kindersl**
Chas Howson / The Trustees of the British Mu
(br); Courtesy of Queens's Rangers (cra); Natio
Constitution Center (c). **22 Getty Images**: De
Agostini Picture Library (cb). **23 Dorling Kinde**
Max Alexander (cb); Courtesy of David Edge (c
Alamy Images: Streetlife (crb). **Dorling Kinder**
B&O Railroad Museum, Baltimore, Maryland, U
(tl); Museum of English Rural Life, The Universi
Reading (tr); The Science Museum, London (cr,
26 Dorling Kindersley: Confederate Memorial
New Orleans, LA (tc). **27 Dorling Kindersley**: P
Keim (c). **28 Corbis**: (br). **29 Dorling Kindersley**
Imperial War Museum (fcr). **Getty Images**:
Popperfoto (bl). **30 Dorling Kindersley**: Imperi
War Museum, London (bl). **Getty Images**: Capt
Poston / IWM via Getty Images (br). **31 Dorlin**
Kindersley: By kind permission of The Trustee
the Imperial War Museum, London (tc); Eden C
Museum, Yorkshire (cra). **Getty Images**: Hultor
Archive (cl); Roger Viollet (c); Sgt. Lou Lowery
MCT / MCT via Getty Images (bc). **33 Corbis**: H
Benser (t); Hulton-Deutsch Collection (b). **34-3**
Getty Images: Gilles Bassignac / Gamma-Rap
Via Getty Images. **35 Corbis**: Masatomo Kuriy
(tl) **35 Getty Images**: Mohammed Al-Shaikh /
(cr). All other images © Dorling Kindersley. F
further information see: **www.dkimages.com**